Lessons From Above

1st Edition

by Kathi Boyle

ASA Publishing Corporation
1285 N. Telegraph Rd., PMB 351, Monroe, Michigan 48162
An Accredited Publishing House with the BBB
www.asapublishingcorporation.com

All Rights Reserved. No part of this publication may be reproduced, stored in a retrieval system or transmitted in any form or by any means electronic, mechanical, photocopying, recording or otherwise, without the prior written permission of the publisher. Author/writer rights to "Freedom of Speech" protected by and with the "1st Amendment" of the Constitution of the United States of America. This is a work of non-fiction Christian education attributes. Any resemblance to actual events, locales, person living or deceased that is not related to the author's literacy is entirely coincidental.

With this title/copyrights page, the reader is notified that the publisher does not assume and expressly disclaims any obligation to obtain and/or include any other information other than that provided by the author, except with permission. Any belief system, promotional motivations, including but not limited to the use of non-fictional/fictional characters and/or characteristics of this book, are within the boundaries of the author's own creativity in order to reflect the nature and concept of the book. Unless otherwise indicated, most scripture quotations are taken from various biblical translations of the Holy Bible.

Any and all vending sales and distribution not permitted without full book cover and this copyrights page.

Copyrights©2025, Kathi Boyle, All Rights Reserved
Book Title: Lessons From Above
Date Published: 09.29.2025
Book ID: ASAPCID2380960
Edition: 1 *Trade Paperback*
ISBN: 978-1-960104-89-2
Library of Congress Cataloging-in-Publication Data

This book was published in the United States of America.

Legal DISCLAIMER

DISCLAIMER: No book will ever replace the Bible!

This book is simply designed to encourage you to read and study the whole story. All dates are based on historical research and are approximate.

All assumptions are made based on my interpretations from my life experience and understanding.

Kathi Boyle

Dedication

It is with a grateful heart that I **dedicate** this book to:

Rev. Timothy A. Thompson, Sr.

for giving me an opportunity to develop and teach Spiritual Enhancement classes for our veterans at Emmanuel House, and to those veterans for their contributions in the classes.

And to:

Deborah Young,

a friend and loving sister in Christ, who keeps putting me in a position of having to present Scripture to the church and for being a wonderful living example of God's love.

Acknowledgments

To **Peter and Joan Yelorda**, *for first introducing me to the faith and encouraging me to study the Bible;*

To my sister, **Anna Lindberg**, *for planting the first seed to write this book;*

To my review team **(Anna Lindberg, Suzanne Moore, Kristopher Boyle, and Alecia Williams)** for tirelessly reading each section as it was developed and giving me their feedback;

To all the wonderful **Emmanuel House Veterans** that attended the classes and contributed so much to my growth, and to **Rev. Timothy Thompson Sr.,** for the opportunity to teach them;

To **Steven Hill, of *ASA Publishing*,** *for all the hours he put in above and beyond the call of duty to produce each of my books and create beautiful covers, and edit their content;*

To **Deborah Glass**, *a wonderful Spiritual mentor and business partner for the past 20 years; and*

Ultimately**, to my God, the Holy Family**, *for it was only with His encouragement, direction, and support that this book would have even been possible.*

It is my prayer that the content will make you want to know more, and the Bible will become your greatest teacher.

!!!Forewarning!!!

There are cautions I need to issue before you read this book:

1) Facts for each chapter come from the Bible and historical writings. The portion of the story that comes from history is approximate. The dates vary with different studies, so I have added the *"Timeline of Biblical History"* map that I have chosen to use at the front of the book. It matches most closely with the majority of my research.

2) The particular people chosen for each chapter were random. As I felt led in my teaching and my devotional studies, certain lessons caused me to stop and think. As there is no end to the lessons the Bible provides, I had to choose just a few. If you read the Bible for yourself, you will find many more lessons that may apply more to you.

3) **I AM HUMAN.** I have made many mistakes in life, and I am sure I have made a few here. It is a huge responsibility to try to explain God's word, and I take this challenge

seriously. It is my hope that you will read each story directly from the Bible for yourself; and know that the information you get from the Bible is always correct.

For the past twenty-five years, I have made it my mission to read through the Bible. Every year, I learn something I missed in prior readings. The Bible is alive and speaks to us when we are ready to hear. It is my goal with this book to whet your appetite enough to make you want to read the stories for yourself. There is nothing quite like going to the original source to get all the facts accurately.

May God bless your reading and open your heart to all He has to offer you.

Love in Christ,

Kathi Boyle

Foreword

TRINITY

It is a human term created to describe something we have no ability to completely understand; the concept of a 3-in-1 God of Father, Son, and Holy Spirit. Of the three, the only one visible to man was the Son, Christ Jesus. Although all three are present throughout creation, they are each visible in a different role. The Father's role is to train and discipline the children. The Son's role is to follow the instruction and reflect the character of the Father. The Spirit's role is to guide and direct after the living example is no longer visible. The complete story of the Trinity is told in the Bible. From Genesis through Malachi, we see the Father. From Matthew through John, we see the Son; and from Acts through Revelation, we see the Spirit at work.

The Father

When this world was created, God provided all that was needed to sustain life and provide joy. His crowning creation was man, whom He made in His image. He could have created man, as other creatures, with knowledge and instincts, but no ability to choose. But, without the ability to choose, there would be no worship and no love. Man would simply be another slave for the Master; the creature He chose to keep the earth clean and control the other animals.

(Genesis 1:28 NASB tells us God created man and blessed him and said to him *"Be fruitful and multiply and fill the earth and subdue it; and rule over the fish of the sea and the birds of the sky and over every living thing that moves on the earth."*)

The Father had a choice; man could be His slave, or man could be His son. But for man to be His son, he had to have the ability to love. Love cannot be mandated; it must be freely given. Therefore, man had to have the ability to choose to love or not to love. Those who choose to love his Creator become His children. Not all men will make that choice. Some will choose evil over good. But, for God to take evil out of the world means

He would have to remove choice, which would remove love. Therefore, evil must be removed by man. Man must become the hands and feet of the Lord.

If man chooses a character of kindness, justice, and love, and teaches his children the same, if he treats his family, friends, co-workers, business partners, enemies, and strangers with this same love and sets the example of a loving God, he has done his part to fulfill God's original plan of a sinless world.

When we see injustice and evil, we have an obligation to confront it. If we are not able to do anything about it, we need to make it visible, so someone who can change it sees it. The possibility of evil being removed completely is not likely, but the obligation does not change.

(Hebrews 12:11" *For the moment, all **discipline** seems not to be pleasant, but painful; yet to those who have been trained by it, afterward it yields the peaceful fruit of righteousness."*)

Discipline is painful, but necessary to stop bad behavior. If there are no consequences, there is no change. If we refuse to change, the Father loves us too much to leave us the same; so, He steps in to do the job for us. The one promise He gives us is in Romans 8:28: *"And we know that God causes all things to work together for good to those who love God, to those who are called according to His purpose."* The evil of this world will not win against those who choose the Father.

Throughout the Old Testament, it is necessary for the Father to constantly redirect His children through discipline and removing distractions and temptations from those not following His lead. Wars and destruction make strong points. They make the consequences of misbehavior obvious. But the Father was dealing with a "stiff-necked" people. They were drawn off course easily; **from creation, He left them on their own for 4000 years before Jesus made His appearance.**

The Son

Throughout the Old Testament, God chose to send people and Angels to deliver messages and make His point. But it did not work, so He decided to come Himself. It is hard to understand why He would come as a man, since man is so flawed. But it was the perfect form to deliver His message, for this was the only creature man could relate to on his own level. He came to earth under humble circumstances (not in royal form), so no one could later say He succeeded because of privilege. He succeeded through every adversity. Here is His story in abbreviated form.

History tells us that Christ appeared between 6 BC and 3 BC. He was born under the cloud of an illegitimate son (born of a virgin was not accepted as truth). He was delivered in a stable, because there were no more rooms available in Bethlehem. His birth was announced from Heaven by the creation of a new star; but the only ones to notice it were some lonely shepherds in the field and several wisemen from another country. It took the wisemen about two years to travel to Bethlehem to find him. (Even though the songs and Hollywood say there were three, the number of wisemen is not known.)

At about the age of two, Jesus was taken to Egypt to protect Him from King Herod who wanted to kill Him. Very little is known of His childhood. He returned to Israel at about the age of four, after Herod died. The next view of His life occurs when He is twelve years old and journeys to Jerusalem for the Passover celebration.

At about the age of 30, He appears again as He is baptized by John the Baptist in the Jordan River as an example for all who want to repent their transgressions and follow

God's lead. It was then He publicly started His earthy mission. When we want to build a solid foundation for our children to follow, we must set an example. For the next three years, Jesus is a living example of a loving God.

One of the first examples He provided for us was to choose your associates carefully. He had no perfect people to choose from; so even though the ones He chose were stubborn and hard-headed, eleven of the twelve were faithful and hard-working and truthful, and they were willing to follow in His footsteps and learn from Him.

They watched Him heal the sick and even raise the dead. Jesus always did for people what they could not do for themselves. But He never told anyone to get up and walk unless they were lame, or to see unless they were blind. The lesson here is that we do what we can do, and God does what we cannot. He will never ask of us more than we can give, and He will never give us more than we can bear.

Most of Jesus' lessons were given in parable form: stories that made the lesson He was teaching clear and visible for anyone who wanted to get the message. He used examples they understood and emotions they could relate to. He always met people where they were.

Man is egotistical enough not to want to listen to or learn from anyone they feel is "beneath" them or not as knowledgeable or rich or successful as they are. So, that meant Jesus had to prove His worth by doing what man could not do; restore sight, heal sickness, remove demons, raise the dead. This confirmed His ability and identity to his disciples, but it raised hatred in those jealous of His powers – which eventually led to His crucifixion.

The timeline for His life for most historians was from 3 BC to 30 AD, based on the historical knowledge of the rulers of the time. All of history is now recorded based on the birth of Christ – BC (before Christ) and AD (after Christ). His life changed history.

The Holy Spirit

Fortunately for man, when Jesus returned to the Father, He did not leave us alone. He left part of Himself with us in the form of the Holy Spirit. Once again, we have a choice to invite Him in to live with us or not.

The Spirit brings both knowledge and wisdom. He helps us through every challenge by reminding us of the wisdom Jesus provided. He brings back to mind the lessons we learned by studying God's Word. He gives us the strength to stand up against evil, and He gives us discernment in how to do that. He provides peace through our storms and challenges of life. He is the conscience that helps us to know and do the right thing. He builds our faith; and faith makes all things possible – not easy, but possible.

When we accept the Spirit, we become a temple for God. Our character, our behavior, becomes the living example of the goodness of God. God gives clear instruction, in detail, of how to maintain the temple. Only perfect sacrifices are to come into the temple. Every item in it is clean and well maintained. Everything is done in a timely manner. These are instructions for both the physical temple of the Old Testament and for the living temple in us.

The way we feed ourselves, clothe ourselves, and act toward others must change to reflect the values the Father and the Son portrayed. We must be disciplined and loving. For, if we are not, we are tarnishing God's image. The problem with being a living sacrifice is that we keep crawling off the altar to do our own thing.

Do you doubt?

Throughout the ages, there have always been doubts as to the truth of the Bible. For example, for many centuries Abraham was assumed to be just a story, because the city of Ur was assumed not to have existed – until it was discovered by archeologist. There will be doubts until the end of time, but so many of them have already been removed that it is becoming harder to deny. Many people believe that Jesus was not who He said He was, but all of His disciples went to their graves without ever denying His divinity. Josh McDowell wrote a book, "***More than a Carpenter***", that covers this doubt very well. I highly recommend it.

The Bible says that through the life, death, and resurrection of Jesus the gates of Heaven are open for all those who believe this fact to have eternal life in peace, health, and fellowship with God Himself. If this is in fact true, I think it would be worth looking into. Dr. Larry Crabb wrote a book, "***66 Love Letters***", that will walk you through the Bible; and Ellen G. White wrote "***Steps to Christ***" and "***Desire of Ages***" that cover the life of Christ; and John Ortberg wrote "***Soul Keeping***" that covers the Holy Spirit.

The reward of knowing the truth is great and worth the effort to research. If you have a desire to read through the Bible in a year, Wayne Cordeiro's book "**The Divine Mentor**" is an excellent guide. May God bless your efforts!

Table of Contents

Dedication 3

Acknowledgments 5

Forewarning 7

Foreword 9

A Timeline of Biblical History 23

Lessons From Above

Noah 23

Jacob the Patriarch 33

Joseph, Son of Jacob 41

Moses 49

Deborah 57

Gideon 65

Mephibosheth 73

Elijah 81

Amos 91

Esther 99

John the Apostle 109

Jairus 119

The Apostle Peter 127

Paul 133

After Thoughts 143

Lessons From Above

1st Edition

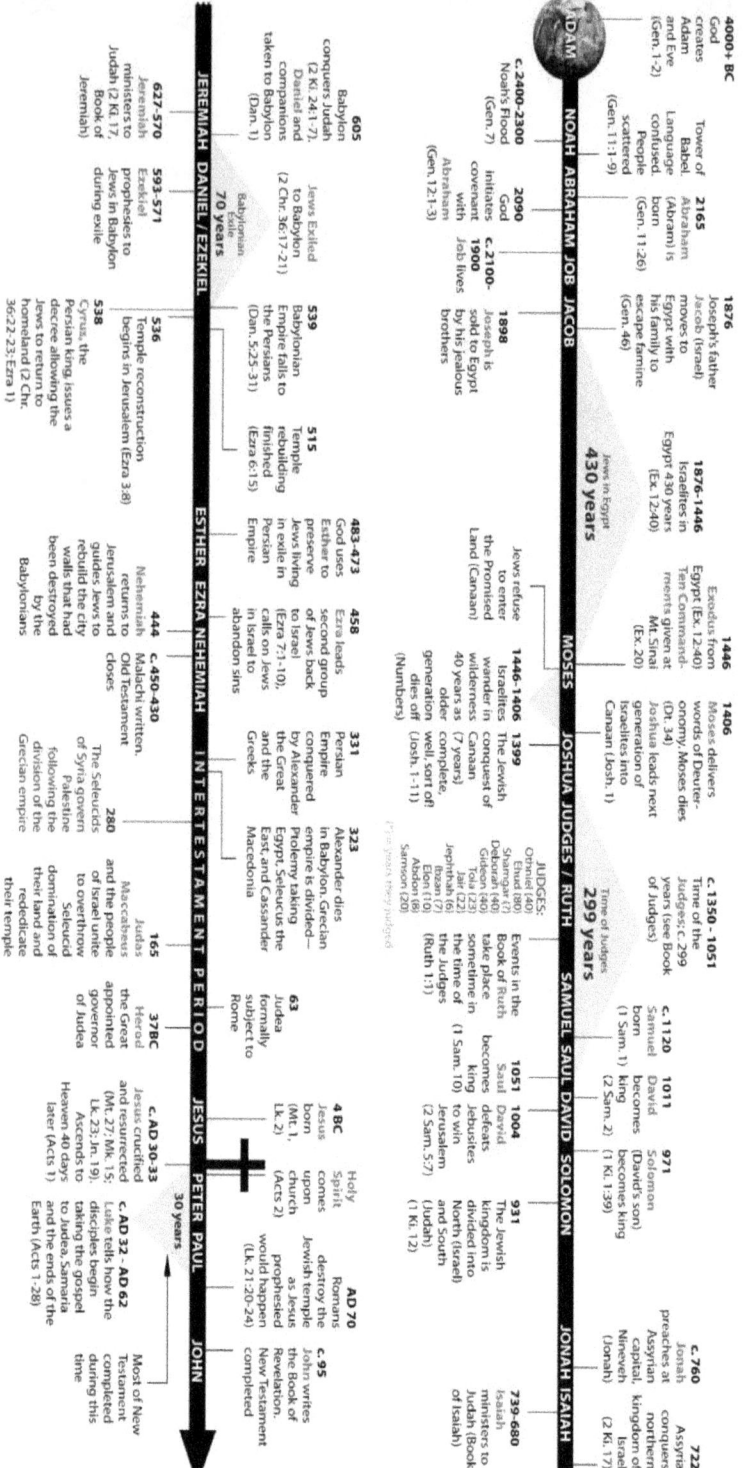

Noah

(Genesis 5 through 9)
(Noah means "peaceful", "rest" or "comfort")
About 2300 BC

Father:	Lamech
Grandfather:	Methuselah
Sons:	Shem, Ham, Japheth
Lifespan:	950 years -10th generation from Adam
Occupation:	Farmer, Shipbuilder, Evangelist, and temporary Zookeeper

We do not know a great deal about Noah except what is in the Bible. History has little to add. We are introduced to Noah at the age of 600 in Genesis 5. The Bible tells us that he had three sons by the age of 500. Whether they were triplets or individual births, it does not say. We also know he took 120 years to build the Ark, as instructed by God, in a secluded area away from water at a time when rain was an oddity; and we know this Ark would save

Noah's family and the animals of the earth.

This means that Noah was working on the Ark many years before his children were born. It is all they knew. They watched their father follow God's instructions from birth. Noah worked day-after-day, week-after-week, month-after-month, and year-after-year for 120 years to accomplish the task God gave him with no visible benefit to him or anyone else. He did not build this boat near water; to the rest of the world, this made no sense. It was a long time to wait; but God made it worthwhile.

We know the reason God had commissioned the Ark was because the men on earth were not following God's lead. They did not believe in Noah's prophecy of a coming flood. Noah was surrounded by unbelievers – people who did not believe in God and did not believe Noah. The Bible says: *"Then the Lord saw that man was very sinful on the earth. Every plan and thought of the heart of man was sinful always."* (Genesis 6:5). It must have been so painful and disappointing for God to look down and see that all the people he had created, the people He loved and cared for, the people He had lavished with Grace and mercy, had turned against him. Were it not for finding Noah to be a righteous man, the earth would have been demolished at that time. But God's heart would not allow Him to eliminate a righteous man.

God expects us to be like Noah, to follow His instructions and obey Him. He expects us to stand up for Him and what is right. He expects us to build and maintain a relationship with Him. He expects us to be a beacon of faith in a world of darkness. No wonder He loved Noah so much. The Bible actually says that Noah was one of three men God acknowledged as most righteous: Noah, Daniel, and Job (Ezekiel 14:14). God honored Noah's faithfulness. Don't be afraid to stand up and be different. To be ashamed or embarrassed of your relationship with God is misrepresenting Him and the joy He provides.

Noah took on a job that required all of his time and focus; he was always paying attention to God's instructions on how to build and on the reward of saving his family and preserving the animals of this world. We find God's detailed instructions for building the Ark in Genesis 6:14-16. Mathematically, this means the three-story boat that would hold about 45,000 animals (according to history) would be about one-and-a-half football fields in length and about 1,518,000 square feet of room.

During all this time, Noah was preaching to the people to turn their lives around so they too could be saved (2 Peter

2:5). Noah warned the world of what was to come, but no one listened. He spoke all during the time he was building (120 years) of the coming of God's judgment. He preached repentance and salvation to a tough audience. It is my assumption that Noah had a heart and a great desire for others to be saved. I think, for that reason, when it was time to close the door of the Ark, God closed it Himself so Noah could not open it; and only the chosen would be saved.

After the doors were closed, God still waited seven days before the rains started – maybe it was one last time for people to repent or an opportunity for Noah and family to recommit to Him; but once the rain started, it rained for 40 days and 40 nights. The entire world was under many feet of water, and every living thing on earth drowned. One-hundred-fifty days after the rain stopped, the waters started to recede. Noah and family spent almost a full year on board.

After the rains stopped, Noah sent out a raven. Sailors until very recent times sent out a raven for direction if they could not spot land, for a raven will head directly to land. If they don't reach it, the sailor will still know which direction to head. When the raven returned, Noah waited and then sent out a Dove. A Dove's flight endurance is shorter, so it would return faster, which meant they had to wait a little longer until it was sent out and did not return – which meant it found land.

According to the Bible, the Ark came to rest on the top of the mountain range of Ararat in what is now Eastern Turkey, far from the carnage left by the flood. It was here that God made a covenant with Noah to never again use a flood to eliminate His creation, and He gave Himself the symbol of the rainbow to remind Himself when we get really bad to not do that again. In other words, the rainbow was a sign by God to God not to flood the world again (Genesis 9:11-13). **The rainbow today reminds us that we have gone so far astray that God has to remind Himself not to destroy us.**

When the Ark finally rested on dry ground, Noah was 601 years old. He celebrated one birthday on board the Ark. He then lived an additional 349 years after landing, to the ripe old age of 950. We have to assume that bodies did not age at the same rate then as they do now, for Noah was a strong, vibrant, virile man ready to start over in life at the age of 601.

There is more to the story, and you will find it in Genesis 5-9.

To Summarize:

- It took 120 years to build the Ark.
- It took time to collect the animals.
- It took time for the rain to start
- It took time for the rain to end.
- It took time for the land to dry.
- It took time for the land to replenish
- It took patience all along the way.
- It took dedication, focus, and faith that it was worth it.
- It took following explicit directions to get it right.
- It took persistence to keep building with no sign that the Ark was needed.
- It took tough skin to not be effected by ridicule from others.

Whatever you are waiting for, it is worth it when the outcome is the perfect will of God.

When God wants a job done, it gets done. We do not know if God offered this request of His to anyone other than Noah. We just know that Noah accepted His request freely. God only wants us to come willingly and follow

His instruction — He will not force His will on us. He will not take away our choice to refuse.

Noah knew God, believed God, and proclaimed God. The people rejected God (and probably Noah), but Noah did not quit. He did not get distracted or discouraged. He never gave up. One-hundred-twenty years is a long time to stay faithful without seeing the result of your efforts. Noah was in the minority. How do we handle waiting?

Today, we are all descendants of Adam, because Noah was. But we are also all descendants of Noah. We each have a choice of how to go forward in this new environment. We have a choice of which path we will follow. Will we remain dedicated, as Noah was? Or will we follow another path?

Noah's story is a story of commitment, focus, and dedication with a reward of peace and prosperity to follow a long life in God's presence. A great example for us. All we have to do is discern the path God has laid out for us and follow it with the same persistence Noah had.

I found this article online and felt it was a great description of **"What We Can Learn from Noah's Life"**:

Noah's life, as recorded in the Bible, offers valuable lessons of faith, obedience, and perseverance. He serves as an example of how faithfulness to God can bring salvation and hope in times of adversity. Here are three important points we can learn from Noah's story:

1. **Unshakable Faith in God**: Noah lived in a time of great corruption and wickedness, yet he maintained his faith in God. Even when faced with the monumental task of building the ark, Noah fully trusted in God.

2. **Absolute Obedience**: When God commanded Noah to build the ark, he followed every instruction without question. Noah's obedience exemplifies how we should respond to God's directions, even when we don't fully understand.

3. **Perseverance in the Face of Difficulties**: The construction of the ark and the wait for the flood required years of hard work and patience. Noah endured ridicule and disbelief, persevering in his mission. His resilience teaches us to stay determined and focused on God's purpose for us.

Noah's story encourages us to **trust in God, follow His call with dedication, and persist through challenges.**

Noah is mentioned in the Bible several times, first in Genesis 5 – 9, then in 1 Chronicles 1:4; Isaiah 54:9; Ezekiel 14:14;

Matthew 24:37-38; Luke 3:36; Luke 17:26-27; Hebrews 11:7; 1 Peter 3:20; and 2 Peter 2:5. You can read it for yourself!

There are many lessons we can learn from Noah and his family. Many doubt the story of the flood, but archaeologists have discovered sea fossils on the tops of every mountain surveyed so far. That certainly makes me wonder, doesn't it you?

Jacob the Patriarch

His story is recorded in Genesis 25 to 49

- Grandson of Abraham
- Son of Isaac and Rebekah
- Twin brother to Esau
- Born (estimated) 1836 BC
- Four wives: Leah, Rachel, Bilhah and Zilpah
- 12 Sons: Reuben, Simeon, Levi, Judah, Dan, Naphtali, Gad, Asher, Issachar, Zebulun, Joseph, and Benjamin
- One daughter: Dinah
- Died in Egypt 1689 BC at age of 147
- Name means "Deceiver"

Jacob is one of those people in the Bible whose reputation changed drastically over his lifetime. He was born into the arranged marriage of Isaac and Rebekah. As the story goes, Rebekah was told she was having twins and the younger would rule over the older. Jacob was born after his brother Esau, holding on to his ankle. From the beginning he wanted to be first. If you read the whole story, you discover how he deceived his brother to gain his birthright and then deceived his blind father into the favored blessing. Granted his mother, Rebekah, was a big part of the deception, but Jacob was the instigator who carried it through.

When Esau discovered his deception, Jacob was forced to leave home in fear of his life. Rebekah sent him to her brother Laban's home in Haran where Jacob gets a taste of his own medicine when he is deceived by Laban.

Jacob falls in love with Rachel, one of Laban's daughters and asks to marry her; agreeing to work seven years for Laban as a bridal gift. Laban agrees but then substitutes his daughter, Leah, instead under the pretense that the older had to marry first; but now he can give Jacob Rachel after a bridal week - if Jacob will work another seven years. Poor Jacob now knows what it feels like to be deceived. In total Jacob worked with Laban for 20 years. He was about 77 when he arrived and 97 before he was able to leave. There are more deceptions to read about in Genesis 31.

When Jacob left Laban, his children were between 6 and 13 years old. He waited until Laban was traveling with his boys and packed his wives and children and all his livestock and left. It took Laban three days to catch up and, if not for God's warning to Laban, that might have been the end of Jacob.

Jacob had a salty reputation; but on his trip home he had a chance to look in the mirror. Jacob knew he had a battle on his hands when he met Esau, his brother, again as he was sure Esau could not be happy for his return. That night he spent time alone at the River of Jabbok where he met his God face-to-face. He fought with God and was tenacious refusing to let go until he received a blessing. My feeling is that the blessing he was hoping for was forgiveness. In the end, the "angel" wrenched his hip with a permanent limp as a future reminder of the battle and let him go. The word Jabbok means "wrestle".

On the banks of Jabbok, Jacob wrestled in the mud with his own conscience, his own mistakes. (Gen 32:24-30) Because he was sincere, God not only gave him his freedom, He gave him a new name – Israel – for his sons are to build the tribes of the nation of Israel for Him. This is a good lesson for all of us. We have all wrestled with our conscience from time to time. Jacob is a good example of coming face-to-face with our wrongs and admitting them so we can make a change.

Jacob was not the only one to wrestle. There are many stories in the Bible of men wrestling with their mistakes and coming back from them when they turned to the Lord.

- David wrestled after Bathsheba
- Samson wrestled after Delilah
- Elijah wrestled after Jezebel with the "still quiet voice"
- Peter wrestled every time he heard the cock crow.

What are you wrestling with? Facing our issues with the promise that they will be forgiven is freeing. Whether we admit our wrongs or not, our deeds have a way of finding us – if not with man, certainly with God. What we do with them when they do will change our lives for the better or for the worse. So, what do we do?

- Do we make excuses?
- Do we brush it off as not important?
- Do we try to escape responsibility?

After wrestling all night, the next morning, Jacob went back across the river and receives the news that Esau is coming to meet him with 400 men. In the hope of warding off a massive killing, Jacob broke his family up into four divisions (one for each wife) and sent them off with gifts for Esau in the hope of appeasing him. Jacob is forced to either retreat or face his brother as he faced his God. Maybe he was tired of running. Maybe he was really sorry. Or maybe he was just tired. But this time he did not run.

When he finally met Esau, the reunion was peaceful – not at all what Jacob expected. Very possibly both brothers realized they had a part to play in their conflict. It appears that Jacob's mother, Rebekah, may have already passed away and Isaac was an old man. Both men were now wealthy in their own right, so they let bygones be bygones.

Jacob had fought with his God and received his blessing, but he did not immediately change his life. If you read his full story, you find that he was not a good father. He had very rebellious boys and many conflicts with his wives. He favored his son Joseph, which led to rebellion in the family. His story starts in Genesis 25 and ends in Genesis 49. To read the whole story is like reading a novel of the good, the bad, and the ugly.

Jacob chose to separate from Esau and moved on to Succoth and then to Shalem and Bethel. On the way from Bethel to Bethlehem, Rachel dies in childbirth to his last son,

Benjamin. Jacob then moves the family to Mamre to be near his father, Isaac, before he dies. Jacob would have been about 108 at this time and lived in Mamre for 12 years, and he ended up in Egypt with his son, Joseph, when the famine hit the land.

When our sins catch up with us, we can do one of two things – wrestle or run!

Max Lucado said, "*We, too, should cross the creek alone and struggle with God over ourselves . . . We, too, should unmask our stained hearts and grimy souls and be honest with the one who knows our most secret sins.*" Max Lucado has many great books that will help lead us in the direction of appreciating the love and forgiveness of God.

All of our actions have consequences. Some good and some bad. What is the old adage: *Play today and tomorrow you will pay*? God is willing to wrestle with any of us who are willing to wrestle with Him. He will win, but the battle will be worthwhile. God can change anyone who is willing to change. Our past is a learning tool. God made the past so we would have a place to bury our mistakes. To ignore our wrongs is to miss our lesson.

What does your future hold:

- Will you let go and let God?

- Will you be open to forgive, so you can be forgiven?

- Will you accept the consequences of your actions – even if it requires a limp?

- Will you make the changes you need to make?

According to 1 Thessalonians 5:18, where you are right now is what God has willed for your life. If you are where you do not want to be, it is very probably a result of decisions you have made along the way. We often find ourselves in bad places because of our own decisions or because of our reactions to someone else's wrong actions.

What are some of the lessons we can learn from Jacob's life decisions?

- You are right where you are supposed to be.

- God has a plan for your life, and it is to prosper you not to harm you. (Jeremiah 9:11)

- God does not lie. He promised that the younger would rule over the older. It was not necessary for Jacob to steal the birthright. But by doing so, he suffered.

- God can turn any situation around. He can make a father-in-law leave you alone. He can make a brother forgive you. He can bless you even when you misbehave.

- You cannot out sin God's forgiveness.

- He sings over you. You are His child!

BE GRATEFUL!

"The way to get started is to quit talking and begin doing."

Walt Disney

Joseph, Son of Jacob

Joseph's story is found in Genesis 20:24 to Exodus 1:6

The People:

- Father: Jacob
- Mother: Rachel
- Uncle: Laban (Mother's brother)
- Grandparents: Isaac & Rebekah;
- Great grandparents: Abraham & Sarah
- Step-Mothers: Leah, Bilhah, and Zilpah
- Brothers: Reuben, Simeon, Levi, Judah, Dan, Naphtali, Gad, Asher, Issachar, Zebulun, Benjamin
- Sister: Dinah

Joseph was one of twelve sons of Jacob, the son of Isaac, the son of Abraham. He was born of Jacob's wife, Rachel, in Padan-Aram about the year 1880 BC. His father, Jacob, at the time, was about 90 years old. When Jacob and family returned to Canaan, Joseph would have been about six years old. They moved from Padan-Aram to Shalem, and from Shalem to Bethal, and from Bethal to Bethlehem.

His last brother, Benjamin, was born outside of Bethlehem where his mother, Rachel, died in childbirth. Joseph would have been about seven or eight years old at the time. Joseph was the eleventh son for Jacob from four different mothers. This led to a truly dysfunctional family.

Joseph, being the first-born of the favored wife, was spoiled by Jacob, and as a result, his brothers did not like him very much. Jacob was so obvious in his prejudice toward this son that he made him a "coat of many colors" that made him stand out even more. This was the last straw for the brothers. He became obnoxious to them and was resented by the other mothers.

As Joseph reached his teen years, he began to dream. He dreamed that he would be the head of the household and all in the house would bow down to him. He was not smart enough to keep these dreams to himself; and as a result, the brothers resented him even more and started to think of ways to get rid of him.

One day, Jacob, not recognizing the tension in his family, sent Joseph out to find his delinquent brothers who were tending to the sheep. When the brothers saw him coming, they saw their chance to get even. Rather than welcoming him, they attacked him, and Simeon put him in a pit to perish. After some discussion, they decided that rather than kill him, they would sell him to some slave traders passing buy on their way to Egypt for twenty pieces of silver. Ruben, apparently not with them when they made the sale, came back to rescue him, but he was too late. Joseph would have been about seventeen and his brothers between seventeen and twenty-four.

The more they thought about how to explain Joseph's absence, they decided to take his coat which they had saved, kill one of the sheep, dip it in the blood and rip it apart. Then they could tell Jacob that Joseph had been killed by a wild animal. Unfortunately, this story did not relieve the brothers of guilt, as we will see many years later in the story.

The brothers return home, and Joseph is taken to Egypt as a slave. He is taken to a land where he did not speak the language and had no way of freeing himself. In the slave market, he was sold to Potipher, a prominent Egyptian. After a time of service, Joseph proved himself to be so trustworthy that Potipher put him in charge of his whole household.

According to scripture, Joseph was a handsome young man, and Potipher's wife was attracted to him. On a daily basis, she tried to tempt him to "lay with her" and Joseph refused on the basis that he could not "sin against God". At one point, she attacks Joseph, and he pulls out of her hands leaving his coat behind. When Potipher returns, she accuses Joseph of attacking her, and Potipher has him thrown in jail. It is interesting. in a case like that in that era, Joseph would have been killed for that transgression - not put in jail. It makes us wonder if Potipher actually believed his wife; but was in an embarrassing position if he did not.

Once again, even in jail, Joseph's character was so exemplary that it caused the prison guard to put him in charge of all the prison activities. During his incarceration, two prominent men were also imprisoned. One was the cupbearer for the Pharaoh and the other was the Pharaoh's baker. In their sleep both had dreams that they could not interpret. (The Egyptians thought all dreams were messages; and not to understand one was frustrating and scary.) Joseph was able to analyze the dreams, and his interpretation turned out to be true. His one request as the men were leaving the prison was that they would think of him and ask the Pharaoh to get him out of jail since he was innocent. The cupbearer agreed to do that; but unfortunately, when he was free, he forgot all about Joseph for two years.

Two years later, the Pharaoh has a dream that no one could interpret and the cupbearer remembered Joseph. Joseph was then cleaned up and sent to the Pharaoh to answer his questions about his dream. His dreams indicated that Egypt was about to have seven years of prosperity to be followed by seven years of famine. Joseph advised the Pharaoh on how to handle the seven years of famine, and Pharaoh removed him from prison and put him as second in charge of the country next to him.

While in Egypt during the years of feast, Joseph was married to Asenath and had two boys, Manasseh and Ephraim. He was given the Egyptian name of Zaphenath-Peneah and dressed and groomed as an Egyptian – which meant he no longer looked like a Jew. His head would have been shaved, and his face made up to be in the presence of the Pharaoh.

When the famine came, it hit all countries, including Canaan where his family lived. When Jacob's family was running out of food, he sent his sons to Egypt to buy from the storehouse that Joseph had set up. The brothers did not recognize Joseph. They did not even know that he was still alive; but Joseph recognized them. During the years of his enslavement, Joseph had stayed faithful to his God. Revenge was not part of his nature. On the other hand, the brothers had a lot of time to think of their actions and to feel their guilt, especially watching their father's grief, which over the long period changed their character. To get the full story read Genesis 20:24 to Exodus 1:6.

On the second trip to Egypt, Joseph reveals himself to the brothers and offers the family a place in Egypt through the famine. Jacob, with great joy, moves his family to Egypt. There is no indication he ever knew what his sons had done. They all lived in Egypt and Jacob died there. Apparently, the brothers thought that Joseph would wait until Jacob died to take his revenge. But when they apologized and offered themselves as slaves to Joseph, Joseph answered and said: *"You meant it for evil, but God used it for good."* Saving his family saved the Jewish nation.

Some lessons we learn from this story:

➢ No enemy is more threatening than inconsistent parenting.

➢ No response is more cruel than Jealousy.

- Never underestimate the evil pull of revenge.
- No action is more powerful than prayer.
- During the waiting period, trust God without panic.
- Lengthy affliction should not discourage us or change our character.
- God puts us where He wants us to be.
- God is with us in good times and in bad.
- To move forward, forgiveness is essential.
- Betrayal did not keep Joseph from forgiving. He did not become bitter; he became better.
- No matter what others plan, God will make it good.

In every position Joseph served in, he served for God not for man. He had patience in his tough times and never changed his character when he was treated unfairly. He did not fall into temptation, and he did not let power go to his head. His gift of dreams led him into slavery; and slavery led him into leadership. God had a purpose for his life that no one recognized until years after it was accomplished.

Joseph taught us to never compromise integrity even when tempted "day by day". God had a covenant to be with

Joseph that extends to all His children. When we live according to God's design, we, too, are blessed by Him.

Moses
Approximately 1525BC – 1406BC
(Exodus 1 through Deuteronomy 33)

- **Grandfather: Kohath**
- **Father: Amran**
- **Mother: Jochebed (or Jocheved)**
- **Brother: Aaron**
- **Sister: Miriam**
- **Wife: Zipporah (or Tziporah), a Midianite**
- **Father-in-law: Jethro**
- **Sons: Eliezer and Gershom**

So much has been written on the story of Moses that I am not sure there is much I can add to it. So, I encourage you to read it for yourself. You will find it in the Bible from Exodus 1 through Deuteronomy 33. What I would like to focus on is some of the lessons this story teaches us.

It was the original transgression of Adam and Eve that led to the culmination of the Jewish nation being enslaved in Egypt for 400 years. The evil just continued to multiply. God was constantly being put in a position of having to redirect and protect His people. Over and over again, God had to move the Hebrew nation for it to survive: First, with Noah by removing all transgressors; then Abraham is separated from his home; then Jacob is pushed out of his; and finally, Joseph is sold into slavery by his own brothers. Each move grew the nation and put it in a position to secure the Promised Land. It was one transgression after another over the years that put the nation in a position to be enslaved and put Moses in a position to fulfill his mission in life. God has a plan for every life He creates. We come with gifts, talents, and abilities. We come with a purpose, just as Moses did.

Years after Joseph and his accomplishments for the Egyptian nation were forgotten, a new Pharaoh came into power who was threatened by the size of the Hebrew population and chose to crack down on their growth by killing all of their newborn boys. Through God's grace and provision, Moses was spared. You can read about this in Exodus 1.

From his birth in Egypt, to his calling from God, to performing the plagues, through the trip in the wilderness, to the Promised Land, God was with Moses. Every step of his life leaves a lesson for us. Moses is a great example of persistence, tenacity, self-discipline and determination; a great leader and a great example for us to emulate. If we can learn to follow in the footsteps of the successful, we can learn from their mistakes and not have to make the same ones ourselves. So, let's see what Moses has to offer in the way of advice:

- One of the most obvious lessons from Moses was that when God has a plan, no one else - including Pharaoh – can stop it. Moses was saved by Pharaoh's daughter from the Nile and then raised in the royal family, which taught him how to relate in that society. He was then sent to the hill country to herd sheep, so he could later lead people. All along the way, God provided him with people to protect him (his sister, Miriam, watched over him until Pharaoh's daughter rescued him). God supported him by sending his brother, Aaron, to speak for him (Exodus 4:14). And when his mission was ended, God even provided Joshua to take over for him. God knows what He is doing.

- All of Moses' complaining and excuses did not alter God's

plan for him. It is best to submit quickly, knowing that God will provide all you need to succeed at whatever job He gives you to do.

- Miracles come from God. The people of Egypt saw many miracles through Moses, but none of them were done by Moses. God can use us for mighty things, if we will allow Him to. Be open to His direction.

- When you are following God's plan, you have to deal with some stiff-necked people. Opposition is inevitable. Success breeds jealousy, as we see in his siblings of Aaron and Miriam in Numbers 12:10. But it does not alter God's plan. Be prepared to work through adversity.

- God provides all our needs. He met the Hebrew's needs even when they did not deserve it – even when they were unfaithful and complaining, and rebelling against Him. Work hard to stay focused on God's plan for your life. Don't be distracted by your surroundings. Daily study is a good place to start.

- There are consequences for bad behavior. Not anyone who was over 20 years when the Jews left Egypt were allowed to set foot in the Promised Land, with the exception of Joshua (who may have been under 20 at the time of departure) and Caleb. Even Moses was not given that privilege because of his transgression. These rules apply to us, too. God expects us to obey. But He does ensure that Heaven is open to God's faithful.

- Moses allowed anger and frustration to lead him astray. He took advantage of his close relationship with God by taking credit for God's work. By doing this, he ran the risk of leading others astray. That action had to be publicly addressed. God had to show that there are no exceptions to the rule of how He is to be treated. As harsh as this sounds, we know that even though Moses missed the Promised Land, he did gain Heaven, as he appeared with Jesus on the Mount of Transfiguration as a representative of all of us who will die before Christ returns.

If Moses taught us anything, it was how important and rewarding a relationship with God is. Moses spent so much time with God that his face would shine to the point he had to wear a veil for others to be able to look at him. His contact was face-to-face with God. A relationship with God does not mean no mistakes or an easy-going life. It simply means, if you fall, God picks you up; if you transgress and ask, you get forgiveness. Faith makes things possible, not easy.

After 400 years of bondage, the Hebrew people prayed to God: **Exodus 2:²³ *In the course of those many days the king of Egypt died. And the people of Israel groaned under their bondage, and cried out for help, and their cry under bondage came up to God. ²⁴And God heard their groaning, and God remembered his covenant with Abraham, with Isaac, and with Jacob. ²⁵ And God saw the people of Israel, and God knew their condition.*** And God answered their prayer by sending Moses to lead them out of slavery: **Exodus 3:⁹ *And now, behold, the cry of the people of Israel has come to me, and I have seen the oppression with which the Egyptians oppress them. ¹⁰ Come, I will send you to Pharaoh that you may bring forth my people, the sons of Israel, out of Egypt."*** And God assured Moses that the people would believe him, but He did not promise they would obey him. Then God told him, Pharaoh will not listen to you: **Exodus 4:²¹ *And the Lord said to Moses, "When you go back to Egypt, see that you do before Pharaoh all the miracles which I have put in your power; but I will harden his heart, so that he will not let the people go.*** Moses is in for a battle.

From beginning to end of the Exodus, we see the people falling back into the slavery mindset. After 400 years of slavery, they had lost their connection to God. It is highly unlikely they would have had the Sabbath off to worship. It is very likely they felt they had been abandoned by God. So, Moses had a challenge before him of showing them just how powerful God is and how determined He is to fulfill His promise to free them. It took powerful miracles to point them in the right direction.

We also complain. We get so comfortable with our discomfort that we would rather stay where we are than risk a change. But if we are willing, we too can be led to the Promised Land. We too can fulfill the plan God has for us. We, too, can reap the rewards of having God as our friend.

Deborah

A Judge in Israel (see Judges 4 and 5)

- Lapidoth: Husband
- Barak: Deborah's general
- Jabin: Canaanite King
- Sisera: King Jabin's general
- Heber: Descendant of Moses' Brother-in-law
- Jael: Heber's wife

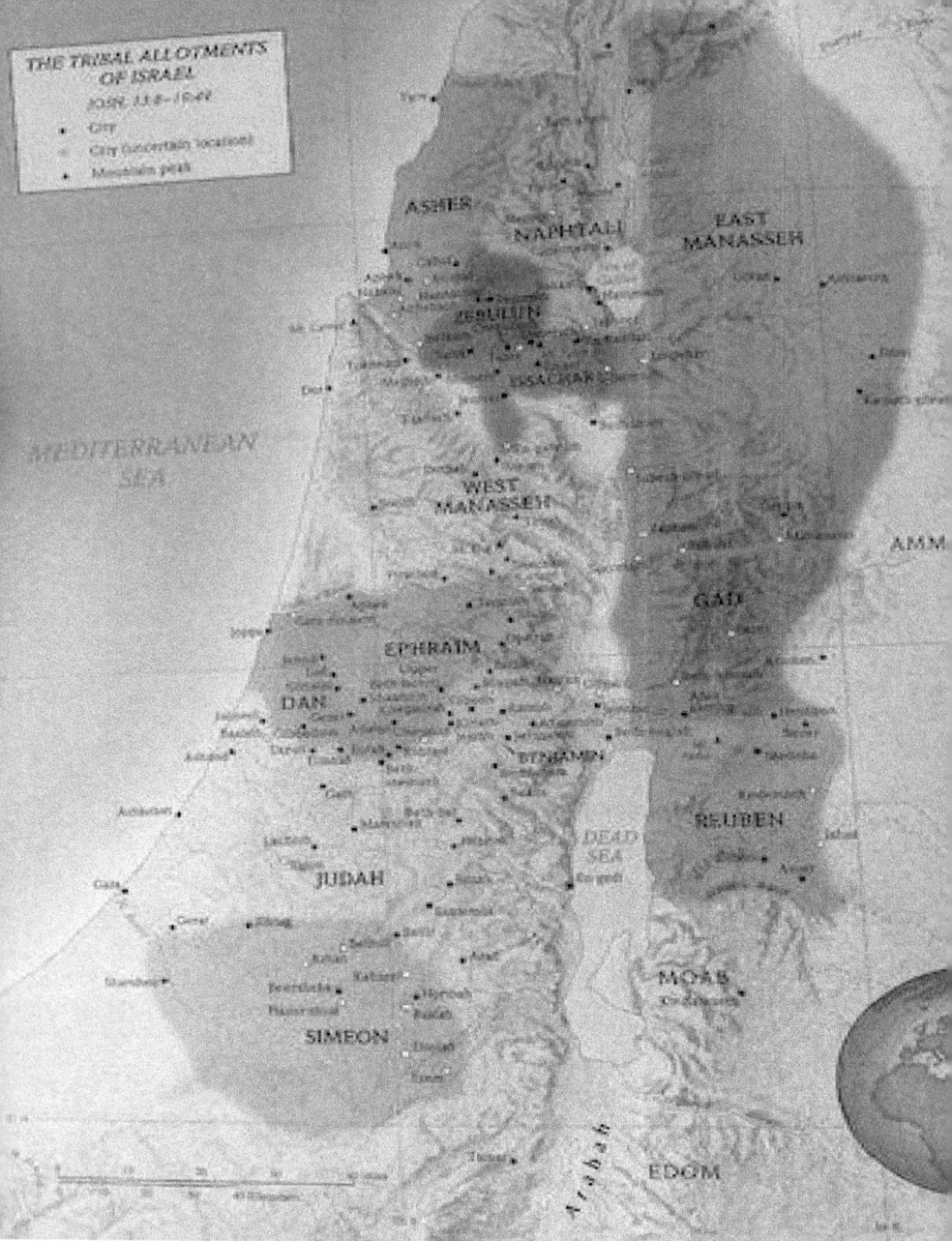

Deborah's story takes place in the Promised Land during the time of Judges. The period of Judges was from approximately **1350 BC to about 1051 BC**.

Deborah is the only female Judge of Israel and the only judge to be called a prophet. A prophet is one who speaks for God. She was one of five female prophets listed in the Bible: Miriam, the sister of Moses; Huldah; Isaiah's wife; Noadiah; and Deborah. Historically, she ruled from about 1190 BC. She was the wife of Lapidoth and lived in the land between Ramah and Bethel, a central spot north of Jerusalem. The children of Israel came to her for judgment under the palm tree named "the palm tree of Deborah".

History of the Jews:

Before Deborah arrived on the scene, the Jews had been enslaved in Egypt for 400 years before God sent Moses to free them. During that time, they had lost their ability to worship freely. They were not able to keep the Sabbath. They were subjected to hard labor, and they were tired. Because they were weak and tired, God led them the long way through the desert for about two years before they reached the edge of the Promise Land. The trip that typically would have taken about eleven days would take them through a path of conflict they were not ready to face.

Unfortunately, when they reached the Promised Land, they

still were not ready to fight, and they refused to enter. Because of their disobedience, God did not allow any of the original slaves who were over 20 years old when they left Egypt to enter the land, other than Caleb and Joshua; so, He kept them In the desert for forty years until they all passed away.

During his time in the desert, Moses trained a successor, Joshua, and it was Joshua that led the people into the land of Canaan. But Joshua did not train a successor for himself. The Hebrews followed God's lead until Joshua's death. After Joshua died, they lost their way. They failed to follow God's command to rid themselves of all the current inhabitants and brought other gods from those people into their worship.

After Joshua, God sent judges to lead. First was Othniel, Caleb's nephew and son-in-law. Then Ehud, Shamgar, and Deborah, who was the fourth Judge and the only woman. Israel was ruled by judges for 325 to 350 years before Saul was set as king.

Deborah ruled from 1107 BC to 1067 BC:

The Hebrews had been instructed by God to eliminate all those living in the land when they took over so there would be no other gods to compete for their attention as they had when in Egypt; but they failed to follow God's orders and left many people in place. Because of Israel's disobedience, God allowed the Canaanites to oppress them for twenty years. It was those people who were not uprooted that came up against Israel as they tried to claim the land. The Canaanites were their biggest opposition. It was through Deborah that God freed the Jews from the Canaanite rule.

He told Deborah to send Barak to Mount Tabor with 10,000 troops to fight against the Canaanites who were ruled by King Jabin whose captain was Sisera. Barak was to gather his troops from the tribes of Naphtali and Zebulun (two of the twelve tribes of Israel). They were a group of foot soldiers going up against a vast army of 900 chariots. It was obvious from the beginning that the win would only come through God.

When Deborah gave the assignment to Barak, his response was that he would only go if she went with him. Deborah was the spiritual leader, and Barak obviously did not have faith in himself to win this war. Was this a sign that Barak knew God was with Deborah; or was he expecting her to refuse to go, thus freeing him from the job? Either way, Deborah consented but told Barak the victory of this war would not go to Barak but to a woman. What woman? Deborah? Or someone else? Let's see.

Deborah Prophet, Judge, Warrior, Poet, Singer:

The battle was to take place at Mount Tabor in the Kadesh valley. Barak set up on Mount Tabor with his 10,000 troops and Sisera set up from below in the valley at Kadesh with 900 chariots and his army. God in His wisdom brought rain that overflowed the rivers in the area, to the point that the chariots were useless. Barak's troops overtook the Canaanites and eliminated all of them except Sisera, who deserts his men and took off on foot and ran.

There was a man named Heber, the Kenite, who was a descendant of Moses' brother-in-law, who had moved his tent away from the other members of the Canaanite tribe. His wife was Jael. When Sisera ran on foot, he ran past the tent of Heber. As he ran past Heber's tent, Jael invited him in. Sisera was tired and thirsty. He obviously thought Jael was loyal to the tribe; he assumed she was a friend. He asked for water. She gave him milk. And he fell asleep.

When he falls asleep, Jael took a tent peg and hammer and drove a peg into his head killing him.

(*Judges 4:21 But when Sisera fell asleep from exhaustion, Jael quietly crept up to him with a hammer and a tent peg in her hand. Then she drove the tent peg through his temple and into the ground, and so he died.*)

THUS, THE BATTLE IS WON BY A WOMAN! Just as Deborah told Barak it would be.

When Barak comes looking for Sisera, Jael shows him where he is. King Jabin is removed and driven out of Israel. Under Deborah's rule, Israel now has peace for forty years.

Israel praises God for the victory (Judges 5:4,5):

Deborah and Barak now compose a song for the Israelites to sing praising God for the victory in battle. You can read the whole song in Judges 5, but this is a little part:

> [4]"*Lord, when you set out from Seir*
> *and marched across the fields of Edom,*
> *the earth trembled,*
> *and the cloudy skies poured down rain.*
> [5] *The mountains quaked in the presence of the Lord,*
> *the God of Mount Sinai—*
> *in the presence of the Lord,*
> *the God of Israel.*"

(Judges 5:4-5)

It is obvious when you are in a battle of this size that only God can win. We sometimes give ourselves credit for winning the small battles, but the big ones obviously belong to God. The Bible is full of stories where the underdog is victorious because he has God on his side.

Lessons from Deborah:

- When God calls, answer. He will not ask you to do anything He won't support.
- To rule takes wisdom and discernment.
- A good judge adds kindness and support.
- It makes no difference how big the enemy, if God is on your side.
- A prophet's predictions always come true, or they are not a true prophet.
- God is still looking for people to step up and step out in faith.
- God works through ordinary people.
- No matter how big the enemy, God wins.
- Don't forget to say, "thank you".

If you read Deborah's story in Judges 4 and 5, you will find many more lessons that may apply more to you. She was a remarkable woman in history.

Gideon

(also known as Jerubbaal
which means "let Baal defend himself")
From Judges 6 through 8
Gideonn ruled from about 1150 BC to 1110BC

- **Father: Joash**
- **Tribe: Manasseh**
- **Servant: Purah**
- **Oppressors: Midianites**

Gideon was the youngest of a very large family. His father had multiple wives and 70 sons. He lived in Israel at a time when it was being constantly attacked by the Midianites. When the Israelites moved into the Promise Land, God had told His people to get rid of the inhabitants who were worshiping false gods; but Israel failed to follow God's instruction and now they are paying the price. For seven years in a row, the Midianites attacked Israel with a horde of camels and soldiers "more numerous than sand" on the seashore, taking all the food and animals and leaving the Israelites to starve.

When Israel knew the Midianites were on the way, they hid in caves and the mountains to preserve their lives and prayed for God to send help. In His mercy, God sent a prophet to the great tree of Ophrah which belonged to Joash, Gideon's father. The prophet was sent to inform the people of their transgressions.

At the time, Gideon was hiding in the wine press thrashing out wheat for the family. Gideon's family were idol worshipers, but Gideon obviously believed in God; he believed in God, and he was frustrated with Him. God sent a prophet to inform Gideon that God considered him a hero, and he was to lead the Israelites to defeat the Midianites, assuring him that God would be with him.

Even in his belief, Gideon had questions. He asked why, if God is so concerned about Israel, has He let this happen? This does not appear to be the same caring God that brought Israel out of bondage from Egypt. Gideon needs a sign; so, he builds an altar, prepares a sacrifice, and presents it to the prophet. The prophet touches it with his staff and the sacrifice is consumed. But this is not the end of Gideon's request for proof that this message is from God. This is a big battle, and he has to know that this is truly a mandate from God. He prays for God to make the fleece wet and the ground dry and then reverses the request for the fleece to be dry and the ground wet. You can read this part of the story in Judges 6:36-40.

God is patient, grants the request, and then gives His orders. Gideon is to show his dedication to God by destroying his father's alter to Baal and cutting down the Asherah pole and use it for fire to consume the bull he is to sacrifice to God on the altar. Gideon follows the orders but does it at night, so he does not get caught as he is afraid of the people.

When he is discovered, the people approach his father, Joash, and demand he bring his son out to be killed for the desecration of Baal's alter. But his father refused for he said, if Baal is a god, he can defend himself.

Once Gideon is convinced that his message is from God, he proceeds to gather an army of 32,000 soldiers from the tribes of Asher, Zebulun, Naphtali, Manasseh, and Issachar, and he led them to camp at the spring of Herod.

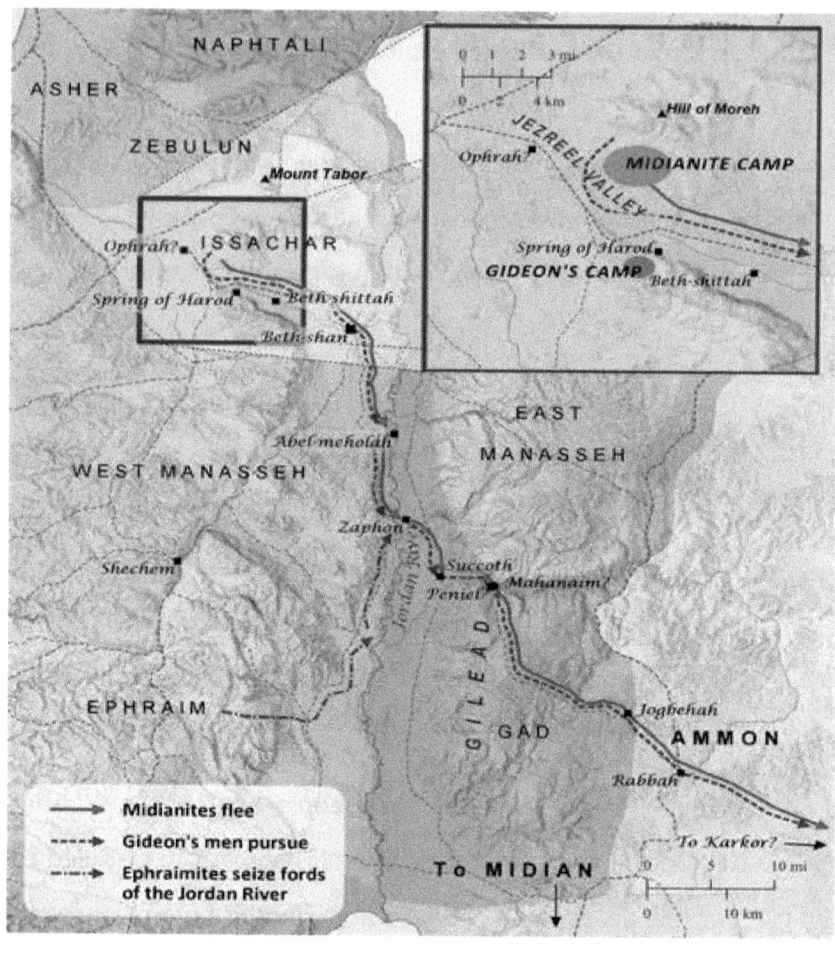

It was not long before the armies of Midian, Amalek, and the people of the east gathered to attack Israel. There were about one million soldiers with the Midianites. They were a mighty group of warriors seeking to destroy Israel. Gideon went with his 32,000 soldiers to meet them at the spring of Herod.

As Gideon is preparing for war, God informed him that he had too many soldiers. **Too many?** 32,000 vs. 1,000,000? Only God could call this "too many". God had Gideon put the soldiers through several tests. Any soldier drinking water with his face in the water is to be sent home. If he laps from his hands, with his eyes focused on everything around him, he is to stay. With several test, God dwindled his group of soldiers down from 32,000 to 300 (300 vs. 1,000,000) and gives Gideon a strategy to follow.

First, He builds Gideon's belief by sending him in to hear the conversation of the Midianite army and finds that they have had a dream that Israel will defeat them. He was allowed to take his servant, Purah, with him so he is also encouraged. The two of them go back to their 300 soldiers and encourage them, laying out the plan God has given Gideon and assuring them that God is with them.

Here is the plan God gave Gideon:

- Divide your 300 soldiers into three camps of 100 each;
- Give each man a trumpet, a jar, and a torch;
- Station the soldiers around the Midianite camp; and, at My direction,
- Have them blow the trumpet, break the jar, light the lamp, and shout.

Gideon follows God's orders and attacks at night. The Trumpets put the fear of God in the Midianites. They are surrounded with trumpet sounds and have no idea how many soldiers are after them. They hear the crash of jars and see the lights coming from every direction. In their fear and confusion, they start to attack anything near and kill their brothers, while Gideon's army looks on. Very few escaped.

As the Midianites are racing back home, Gideon calls for help from the tribe of Ephraim to chase them. But, Ephraim, in its pride, is insulted that they were not called to the original battle. Gideon sends them to chase the kings going south and Gideon goes north. When the Ephraimites are successful in killing the kings in the south, Gideon gives them more credit than he gives himself, pacifying the insult they were feeling. As a result, everyone wants Gideon to be their ruler. He refuses on the pretense that "God is your Ruler."

So, what are some of the lessons we receive by studying Judges 6 through 8?

- There are consequences for not following God's orders. He accepts us where we are but cares too much to leave us there.
- Gideon was created for a purpose. God does not create anyone or anything without a purpose.
- It is okay to be scared. God can work with scared.

Gideon was not chastised for being scared. God allowed Himself to be tested to strengthen Gideon.

- God does not always select the strong. He works best in our weaknesses.
- Give others credit for what they do and don't take credit for what God does.
- God's strategy and support beats all odds. Only God can do what God does, and He likes surprising us.
- God's way are not our ways. He always knows what He is doing. It is our job to trust.
- If we humble ourselves and ask, God will help.
- When we think all is lost, God steps in to prove us wrong.

The story of Gideon, told in Judges 6 through 8, lets us know that God is willing to work with us if we will work with Him. There are so many more lessons in this story. I hope you will read it for yourself.

Know that fear is normal. Courage is working through fear. Courage is proof of faith, and without faith we are lost. Fear of the Lord saved Israel, and it will save us, too.

Mephibosheth
(2 Samuel 9, 16, and 19:24-26)

- Saul: First king of Israel
- David: Saul's successor
- Jonathan: Saul's son and David's friend
- Ziba: Servant of Saul and Jonathan
- **Mephibosheth: Son of Jonathan, Grandson of Saul**

Mephibosheth was a minor character in the Bible. He first appears when he is five years old, and Saul and his family are evacuating the castle in fear of David's return to take the throne. It was not uncommon in that era for the successor of the throne to kill all former family members and their friends, leaving no competition as they come in.

In the process of evacuation, Mephibosheth was being

carried by his nurse. As she was running to save her life and the life of her ward, she fell. There was no medical attention at the time that would mend the injuries and, as a result, Mephibosheth was cripple "in both feet" from that day forward. He was moved to Lo Debar and not mentioned again in the Bible until twenty-five years later when David, still thinking about Jonathan, decides he wants to do something for his friend, who dies with his father, Saul. At this time Mephibosheth is about thirty years old and married with a child.

The lessons we learn from this long story come from several different people: Mephibosheth's Grandfather, Saul, his father, Jonathan, his servant, Ziba, and King David, his father's friend; and from Mephibosheth himself.

Saul:

Saul was the first king of Israel. He was appointed by Samuel at God's request. He resisted the assignment originally; but came to be proud and arrogant in the end and jealous of anyone who might challenge his position. When he failed to follow God's orders, God, through Samuel, told him he was to be replaced. Saul was scared, embarrassed, and hurt; and we know those are the three things that bring out the worst in all of us.

Saul became a tyrant. God would tell him what to do and he would only follow the part he wanted to do and make his own rules. He became his own boss. Saul, in his arrogance, allowed himself to be possessed by an evil spirit and jealousy took over his actions. He was even jealous of David, a young shepherd playing the harp to drive out his evil spirit. If you read the story, you find Saul attempted to take David's life more than once.

Jonathan:

Jonathan was Saul's oldest son and in line for the kingship. He was a grown man and a soldier in his father's army when he met David as a teenager. Even though David was Saul's harpist, Jonathan apparently did not meet David until later when he came to the battlefield where the Philistines were threatening Israel and disparaging God through Goliath, the giant of their group. When David challenged and killed Goliath, Jonathan's respect and love for David grew into a beautiful friendship. He was so humble of heart and devoted to God and David that he offered David his robe and crown. He saved David's life when Saul planned to kill him.

Even though David was one of seven brothers, he considered Jonathan his favorite brother. In the end, Jonathan was killed in battle with his father Saul, and David was crowned king.

Ziba:

Ziba was first a servant of Saul and Jonathan and then a servant of Mephibosheth. He had fifteen sons and twenty servants of his own. His loyalty was obviously with Saul. He exited Jerusalem with Saul's family and moved to Lo Debar.

When David was looking for a way to honor Jonathan, he addressed Jonathan's servant, Ziba, asking if there is any family left from Jonathan. Ziba directs him to Mephibosheth and David vows to move Mephibosheth into the castle to honor Jonathan so he can "eat at my table". He then puts Ziba in charge of all Mephibosheth's property for him and his sons to care for while Mephibosheth moves to live with David.

Ziba pretends to be loyal to Mephibosheth. But, when David flees the castle because his son was attempting to take over the throne, Ziba tells David that Mephibosheth has stayed behind because he does not want to follow David. David, in his frustration, then gives Mephibosheth's property to Ziba. In 2 Samuel 19, when David returns to Jerusalem, he discovers that Ziba, not Mephibosheth, is the one who has not been loyal. Since David had decided no one would die that day (and maybe he is not yet sure who is guilty), he simply divided the land between Mephibosheth and Ziba and kept Mephibosheth with him. Mephibosheth told David to give it all to Ziba, all he wanted was David's safety.

Mephibosheth:

We know very little about Mephibosheth except that he must have been much like his father, Jonathan. He remained loyal to David to the end. When David had to leave Jerusalem, and Ziba betrayed him by telling David he was disloyal, Mephibosheth literally did not shave or shower until David returned. David's safety was his main concern. When David wanted to divide his property with Ziba, even though Ziba had betrayed him, he refused to take anything. It was obviously more important to him for David to know he cared than it was to fight for what was his.

Lessons from Saul:

Saul took revenge as his right and became fiercely possessive of his position. Our worst behavior comes when we are embarrassed, scared, or hurt. God makes it clear that we are to follow Him and His rules. When we fail to do that, there are consequences to pay. Saul died in a battle he should have won if he had followed in God's footsteps, and his bad behavior costs his son, Jonathan, his life too.

This is a prime example that we do suffer from our own transgressions, but we also suffer from the behavior of others. To receive our love, God had to give us choice, and some people do not make the right choices. All will be corrected in heaven.

Saul shows us the results of jealousy and pride. No evil spirit can live in you unless you allow him in by leaving your God.

Lessons from David:

David was a teenage shepherd boy that Saul's servants found to play the harp for Saul when the evil spirit attacked him. It is not clear if David was already playing the harp for Saul before the battle with Goliath; but it is clear that Saul did not recognize him as the harpist.

David is now God's Anointed. If you read the whole story, you find that David had more than one opportunity to eliminate Saul. He had motive, opportunity, and power, but would not do it because Saul was "God's Anointed". He left revenge in God's hands and, as a result, he became the next king.

David also showed us that it is never too late to repay a debt, to honor a friend, to show your love and loyalty.

Lessons from Jonathan:

The example we get from Jonathan is his willingness to accept God's will. He turned over his kingship to David for he knew that was God's plan. He was loyal to David, but he was loyal to his father too. He fought with him and for him and even gave his life with him.

We need to have a heart and a friend like Jonathan.

Lessons from Ziba:

Ziba was a swindler out for himself. In most cases if a new king is looking for a long-lost relative of his predecessor, it is to eliminate him. Ziba wanted Jonathan's property and assumed he would get it if he helped David. He is kind to the face while stabbing you in the back. But, instead, David promoted Mephibosheth and moved him into the castle with him. Ziba is now just a servant taking care of Mephibosheth's property.

I think the biggest lesson from Ziba is that most misdeeds get caught.

Lessons from Mephibosheth:

Mephibosheth was humble, grateful, appreciative, and loyal.

He shows all the characteristics of his father, Jonathan. We discern this from his actions not his words. We don't know much about him except that he did not allow his disability to make him bitter, his actions proved he was not greedy, and his mourning for David's situation showed his loyalty.

There is no end to the lessons we receive in the Bible. I hope you will read the story.

Elijah

If you want the whole story about Elijah, go to 1 Kings 17 through 2 Kings 2.

- **Elijah: Prophet in Israel**
- **Ahab: King of Israel**
- **Jezebel: Queen of Israel**
- **Time period: 900 BC to 849 BC**

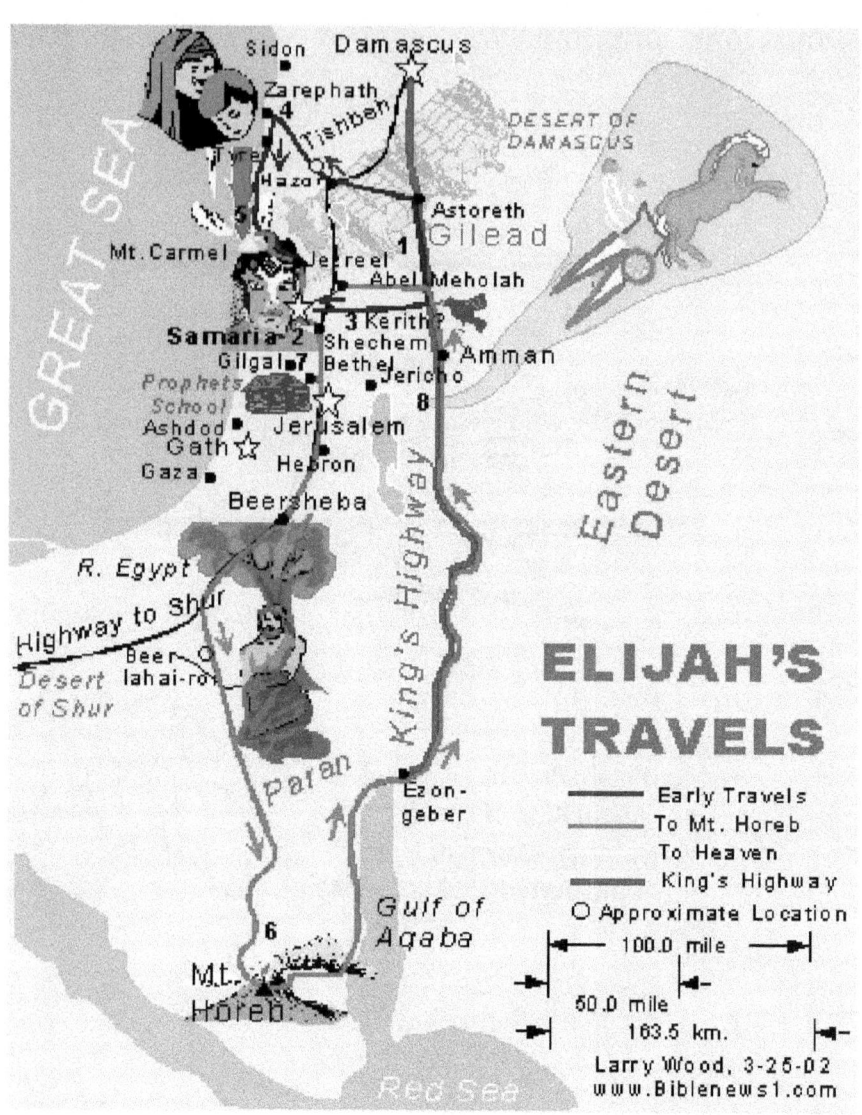

According to most historians, Elijah lived sometime between **900 BC and 849 BC**. The Bible says that Elijah was one servant that God translated to heaven without having to see death; and he is not again seen until he meets in the New Testament on the Mount of Transfiguration with

Moses and Jesus as the representative of those who will be living when Christ returns. Here is his story:

Elijah was a loner who lived during evil times. He lived in caves in Israel and walked everywhere he went. He had to be in wonderful physical condition as you can see from his travel map he was always on the move. It appears most of his time was spent talking to and listening to God; as a result, God was able to use him.

The ruler of Israel at the time was Ahab. Ahab earned the reputation of being the "most evil" king ever to rule Israel (1 Kings 16:30), primarily because of his wife, Jezebel, who imported 850 false prophets into the country. It was because of Ahab's evil that God used Elijah to punish the country.

God sent Elijah to Ahab to inform him He was sending a drought on Israel that would last until Elijah prayed for it to end. God then sent Elijah to Cherith Brook (sometimes recorded as Kerith Brook) out of harm's way. Very probably, Ahab became very worried about Elijah's prophecy when the drought persisted for about three years. By that time, he was angry and looking for Elijah to have him end it; but he was nowhere to be found, for God had hidden him.

Elijah stayed by Cherith Brook and God fed him by sending food through the Ravens and water from the brook. When the brook dried up, God then sent him to Zarephath in Sidon to a widow with a child, who had been instructed to provide for him. This was the place of Elijah's first recorded miracles.

Because of the drought, the widow had run out of flour and oil and was down to making her last meal for her son and herself when Elijah came along and asked her to instead make a cake for him, with the promise that God would provide if she did. Obviously, she had to have believed him, for I doubt seriously she would have provided for Elijah before her son if she did not. By fulfilling that request, she had all she needed to survive the rest of the drought. Sometime later when the widow's son died, Elijah, through the grace of God, performed his next miracle. He took the son, prayed over him three times, and God revived him at Elijah's request.

About three and a half years into the drought, God sent Elijah back from Sidon into Ahab's territory in Samaria, approximately 100 miles walking, to meet with Ahab. Elijah had Ahab summons all of Samaria and all the 450 prophets of Baal and the 400 priests of Asherah that Jezebel had imported into the country to meet him on

Mount Carmel to challenge God to prove Himself to be the real God. (To climb up and back down Mount Carmel is approximately one mile with an elevation of about 1,700 feet.)

Since Ahab needed Elijah to end the drought, he was not in a position to get rid of him quite yet, so Ahab did as Elijah requested. At the top of the mountain, Elijah had the false prophets build an alter to their god, and he built one to his God. An ox was provided for each. The average weight for an ox is about 2,000 pounds. The prophets had 850 people to help prepare theirs. Elijah did it by himself. That is a lot of exhausting work. After begging and pleading all day, the false prophets had no results.

So now it is Elijah's turn. He built an altar, dressed the ox, and dug a trench around the altar. And, using the most precious commodity at that time, water, he drenched the ox until water filled the trench and ran over. He then called on God; and immediately the ox, the alter, and the water in the trench were consumed; leaving no doubt of **Who** is worthy to be praised.

Then the people, at Elijah's command, killed all the false prophets. Now that the prophets have been removed, Elijah is free to pray for rain. He prayed – not once, but seven times before the rains came; but his persistence paid off and a storm arrived. He sent word to Ahab to get down the mountain before the rain prevented him from going. Then Elijah, with the help of God, ran ahead of the chariot to Samaria – obviously elated over the results.

You would think that at this point Elijah would have been full of confidence. He was looking for a "thank you". But Elijah did not get the reception he thought he would receive. He was disappointed by his expectations   Not only was there no appreciation for what he did, but Jezebel threatened his life, and he ran!!! He has just seen the biggest miracle of all time with complete proof that he is worshiping the all-powerful God, and yet he let fear and exhaustion control him. WHY?

Elijah let exhaustion, fear, and doubt take over. He was tired. He had just walked from Zarephath to Mount Carmel 100 miles), climbed Mount Carmel (1 mile elevation), built an altar there, dressed a 2,000-pound ox, been on his knees in prayer, and ran back down Mount Carmel. He was tired from all the walking, climbing, working, and building. He was tired of the drought, and he was tired of the fight God had given him. He was so tired, he forgot to pray. It was like the worst day of basic training. He thought he should be rewarded for his efforts, and he was disappointed; but God's ways are not our ways. There was more Elijah needed to learn. When we move our focus from God to self, we run.

He ran to Beersheba in Judah and again God fed him until he regained his strength to go again. For forty days and forty nights, he walked all the way to Mount Horeb back to a cave. When Elijah got to Mount Horeb, God came to him and said, *(1Kings 19:9) What doest thou here, Elijah?* In other words, "I did not send you here." As is typical of us humans, Elijah starts to defend himself. He informs God that he is the only prophet God has left. I am sure he felt that way. But God informed him that he had 7,000 souls that had not bowed to Baal – Elijah was just one of many.

Elijah is about to learn another lesson. God took him to the top of the mountain, had him stand before Him, and brought on a storm of wind; but God was not in the storm. He then brought on an earthquake; but God was not in the earthquake. He then brought on fire, but God was not in the fire. It was not until Elijah listened to the still, small voice that he heard God. I think God is telling us, you don't rely on being able to hear my presence in the wind, or seeing my power in the earthquake, or feeling the flames in the fire. Even if you do not hear, see, or feel Me, still trust that I am with you In the still, small voice.

There are so many lessons from this part of Elijah's story, and many more in the rest of his story. I highly recommend you study it. Here are a few things I picked up on:

- When we study God's word and spend time with Him, He can use us for His purpose.
- When He uses us, He protects us. Sometimes a dried-up brook is a sign of God's pleasure, and the next journey He wants to take us on.
- We can perform miracles with God's help.
- Persistent prayer pays off.
- There will always be opposition when you are working closely with God.
- God only gives instructions one at a time, and He seldom gives explanations.
- God does not necessarily give easy jobs.

What did Elijah teach us from his experience?

1. When God tells you to do something, do it quickly. He will protect you through it.
2. Know that God is caring for you even when you sleep.

3. When you pray, don't quit until you get an answer.
4. Pay close attention when you are tired or stressed that you don't run away.
5. God knows more than we do.
6. To hear God, you must put yourself in a place to hear a still, small voice.

Elijah continues to follow God and do His bidding until God must have said, "Elijah you are closer to my home than yours". God then provides a replacement for Elijah in Elisha. But when Elijah's job is over on this earth, God made the transition beautiful. He did not have to go through the process of dying. God put him in one of His special chariots and transported him to Heaven. It was not until centuries later, after Jesus' arrival on earth, that Elijah appears again.

On the Mount of Transfiguration, Moses was our representative of a person God allows to die and rise again, and Elijah was our representative of one who is to leave this earth without death. They both appeared with Jesus on the Mount of Transfiguration as a witness to what will happen when Christ returns, and the dead-in-Christ will rise to meet with the living and join Jesus in the clouds of Heaven.

You can find the story of Elijah in 1 Kings 17 – 19 and 2 Kings 2. It is an interesting read full of valuable lessons. May you be blessed.

AMOS

A Minor Prophet

Biography:

- Born in Tekoa, five miles south of Bethlehem.
- A Shepherd and sycamore-fig farmer
- Prophesied from about 760 BC to 755 BC (same time as Isaiah, Hosea, and Joel)
- Assassinated in 745 BC

When Amos lived, the original land of Israel had broken into two divisions: Judah and Israel. Jeroboam II was the king of Israel. He ruled from about 785 BC to 746 BC. The king in Judah was Uzziah, who ruled from about 783 BC to 742

BC. There was relative peace and prosperity in the land at the time of Amos. You will see a map of the main breakdown of countries that God worked, through Amos, to deliver messages on how to get to know Him.

Throughout the Bible you see that you can meet God anywhere. It does not have to be in church. It can be in a burning bush, in the desert, or in an upper room. It can be through a visit from an angel or a prophet. It can be in a still, small voice on the top of a mountain. God is everywhere and can be found if we search for Him with all our heart. He will meet you where you are, but only on His terms, not yours. You cannot meet God without being changed.

All we know about Amos is what is written in his book. History adds very little to his story. He was born in Judah but prophesied in Israel for five years. He was kicked out of Israel because of his gloom and doom preaching about hell and damnation to the countries. When he returned to Judah, he wrote in the hopes of reaching the ears of those God told him to reach. He was eventually assassinated by the High Priest's, Amaziah's, son because he prophesied against his father. All of this is found in the book of Amos in the Bible.

Amos' biggest concern was of the neglect of God's law in how people related to each other. The main message God gave to Amos was that how you relate to each other matters to Him. He was obsessed with the disparity between the rich and poor and the injustice and oppression going on in the countries surrounding him. He had an individual message for each of them.

Amos taught that prayer and sacrifice do not make up for bad deeds. God wants obedience more than He wants sacrifice. He wants fairness and justice above all else, and if any country falls below the moral requirements of God, their relationship with Him will suffer. God's judgment will prevail.

He also preached of God's power and divine judgment that was to come on each country if they did not change their ways and give up their pagan worship. He worked to turn all countries back to the Father.

For each country Amos had a message from God:

Damascus was treating people as things to be used for personal advantage. Amos said this will not work with God. If you are to be His child, you must treat His children well.

To **Gaza** he said, you are not to value financial gain for yourself over the well-being of others. Elsewhere in the Bible God tells us to put others first. He is just repeating His message here through Amos.

Tyre tended to make a promise and not keep it, unless it was in their best interest to do so. Amos said, don't assume your word is breakable just because it serves you. Your word is important to God. It is a sign of your character.

Edom held grudges. They hated people who hurt them. God said, through Amos, that is not your job. Revenge is God's job. Our job is forgiveness. If we do not forgive, we are not forgiven.

Ammon justified their actions. If their actions gave them an advantage, they used them to harm others to get what they wanted. Amos' message to them was, there is no justification in harming others just to create personal satisfaction.

Moab was another violent country. Vengeance was their mode of operation. Once again, Amos had to deliver the message that vengeance belongs to God, not to man. It is not a legitimate right of any man.

But Amos' messages did not end with the countries around him. He prophesied not only to Judah and to Israel, but also to us today.

- To the sins of **Judah**: I will not allow you to disregard my demands and replace them with your standards.

- To the sins of **Israel**: You will not pursue your satisfaction by following a plan for life that does not serve Me first.

- To the sins of **today**: Today's church leads one to believe they can live a self-pleasing life with no inclination to tremble at all.

Although angry with His people in Judah and Israel, and ready to punish the pagan nations around them, God's deepest desire was that they would turn from their sins and repent. It still is. It is the same for us. When we repent, we will be forgiven.

There are many valuable lessons in the book of Amos. It is well worth a read.

Lessons learned.

✓ Actions have consequences.

✓ God reacts to how we treat His children.

✓ God fights for His children (of which you are one).

✓ Mistreatment will not go unpunished.

✓ Poor treatment can be forgiven, if the regret is genuine.

The book, **66 Love Letters** by Dr. Larry Crabb, takes each book of the Bible and explains it through a conversation between Dr. Crabb and God. It is a valuable source of information. After writing this chapter on Amos, I went back and read his synopsis of the messages to each country on pages 150, 152 and decided to repeat it here in the hope that you will also want to read his book. His breakdown of God's message on each countries relational sin is as follows:

- Damascus: *treats people as things to be used for personal advantage.*

- Gaza: *values financial gain for oneself over the well-being of others.*

- Tyre: *regards one's word as breakable when self-interest is served.*

- Edom: *sees nothing wrong with nourishing hatred against people who hurt you.*

- Ammon: *justifies harming others to increase personal satisfaction.*

- Moab: *presumes vengeance is a legitimate personal right.*

- Judah: *disregards the absolutes God reveals as the standard for all relating.*

- Israel: *pursues satisfaction by following a plan for life that is self-serving and not God-glorifying.*

It is obvious God loves His children if He is willing to give us so many chances to turn to Him. God says:

2 Chronicles 7:14 NRSV, *"If My people, which are called by My name, shall humble themselves, and pray, and seek My face, and turn from their wicked ways; then will I hear from heaven, and will forgive their sin, and will heal their land."*

In all of this hell and damnation, God still promises restoration for His people. There is no end to God's grace and mercy, and no limit to His love for His children!

Esther
The Book of Esther takes place between 483 BC and 473 BC.

- King: Ahasuerus (also known as Xerxes) was the most powerful person on earth at the time
- Queen: Vashti – described as beautiful – obviously strong in character
- Hadassah: Also known as Esther, enters the picture in 479 BC. Never underestimate your ability to be used by God right where you are.
- Mordecai: Esther's uncle who raised her – a Jewish man, descended from King Saul, who lived in Persia.
- Haman: Second in Command in Persia: Never underestimate the pull of evil when pride is involved.

The story of Esther takes place in the Kingdom of Persia, a huge territory that has taken over Israel and reaches all the way from India to Egypt. According to history, it consisted of one hundred twenty-seven provinces and covered over two million square miles of territory.

Map of Persia 480 BC

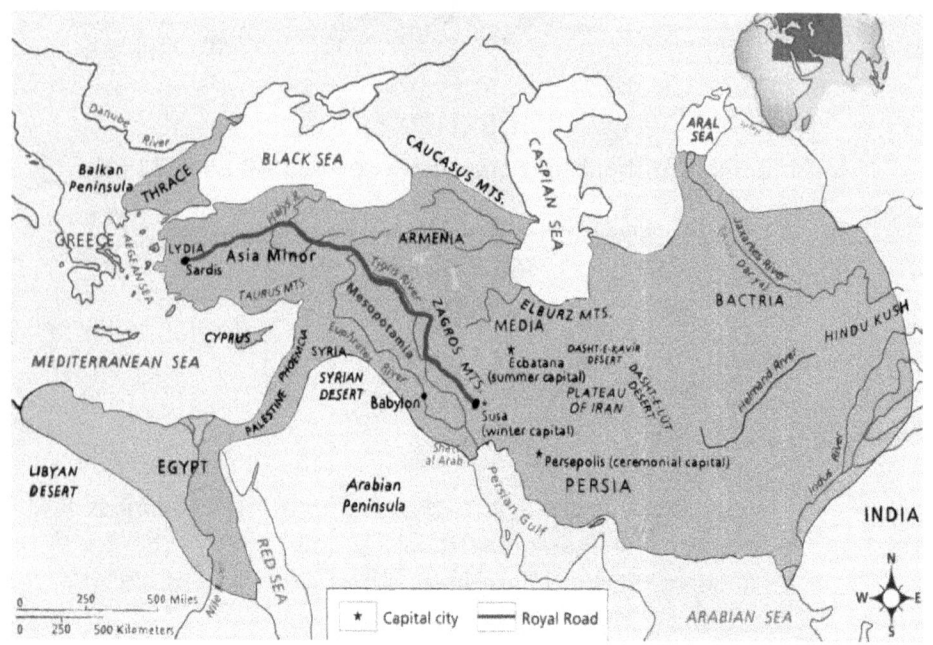

Sometime between 485 BC and 480 BC, Ahasuerus (or Xerxes) attempted to also incorporate Greece into his territory. But he overestimated his importance and abilities and failed in the attempt – something his ego could not tolerate. In the third year of his reign, in an attempt to restore his image, he threw a banquet that lasted about 180 days and consisted of food and drink without limit. At the end of the 180 days, when all the men were drunk on wine and ego, the king decided to parade his wife, Queen Vashti, for all to admire. He uses

Queen Vashti as a pawn for his importance and wants to parade her in front of the drunken crowd, but she refuses to show up. The lessons here: drunkenness creates bad choices; and character is far more important than beauty.

When Queen Vashti refuses to parade for the King, she is vanquished from the kingdom. For two years King Ahasuerus does without a Queen. He has a harem, but he wants a Queen. When he finally admits to his administrators that he has made a mistake getting rid of her, they suggest that he do a kingdom-wide search to bring in all the beautiful women in the kingdom for him to choose a new queen.

All one-hundred-twenty-seven providences were searched – an estimated 2,123,562 square miles according to history. History estimated that about four hundred beautiful young women were found, and Esther (or Hadassah) was one of those women. She would have been twenty years old or younger. She was a Jewish girl who had lost her parents and been adopted by her cousin Mordecai.

Each of the women brought to the palace were given one year of preparation with oils and lotions before being presented to the king. In the end, each woman was given one night with the king for him to select which woman he wanted for his Queen. For a young Jewish woman, this would have been devastating. Had she slept with the King and not been chosen, according to Jewish law, it would have then ruined any possibility of her mating with anyone else. As it turned out, she is the one who pleased the king.

Since Jews were not respected in the Kingdom, her uncle, Mordecai, told her not to reveal her heritage. He then sat at the gate of the castle to watch out for Esther so he would know how she was doing. While keeping his eyes open, he overheard a conversation about an attempt to assassinate the King and reported it to the Castle. The report was documented and the bad guys eliminated, but no recognition was given to Mordecai at the time.

Four years after Esther is made queen, in the seventh year of Ahasuerus' reign, Haman was promoted to second in command. Haman was a self-centered, egotistical man, looking for recognition and demanding respect. But he had a problem. The Jews did not bow to anyone but God – and Haman was not God! Therefore, Mordecai did not bow to him. This irritated Haman to the point that he wanted to get rid of all the Jews in the nation. Haman was an Agagite, a descendant of King Agag. Agag was the king of the Amalekites when Saul was king. Agag was the King that King Saul spared when God told him not to. This story is in 1 Samuel. Haman, as an Amalekite, had carried a prejudice against the Jews from birth.

So Haman plotted to get rid of all Jews and went to King Ahasuerus with a proposal to donate 10,000 talents (or 375 tons of silver) for the king to issue an order to annihilate all Jews in the territory under the pretense that they did not respect the King. Ten thousand talents sound like a great commitment on Haman's part, but he, in fact, expected to regain the funds through the plundering of the Jews.

Once the King made the decree, it was published in all 127 provinces, in the language of each province, that on a certain day, all Jews were to be eliminated without penalty, and everything they owned would go to the person who eliminated them. Needless to say, Mordecai knew this meant ALL Jews. He did not necessarily think about the fact that it also included Esther.

When Mordecai sees the decree, he sends word to Esther to go to the King and request a reprieve. Esther knew that anyone who approached the King without being called would be killed if the King did not reach out his scepter to acknowledge them. So, Esther sends back to Mordecai a request that, before she approached the king, he was to have all Jews praying and fasting for her for three days, and she and her attendants would do the same.

Behind the scenes, God is answering prayer. He keeps the King awake one night. When he can't go to sleep, he has the records of the kingdom read to him and realizes that nothing had been done for this faithful servant who saved his life from an attempted assassination. Early the next morning, he is looking for someone to carry out a command for him to honor "a man the king delights in"; and, low and behold, the only one available was Haman; Haman who had spent the night putting up a seventy-five-foot gallows to impale Mordecai because Mordecai would not bow to him.

When Haman is called to the king, the king asked him what he should do to honor this man. Thinking "this man" was himself, Haman gives his advice and then is told to carry it out for Mordecai. How humiliating! Read the story in the book of Esther.

That same afternoon, Esther goes to the King and makes her

request. Whether it was the request she intended to make or one she diverted to for time, we don't know. But instead of asking for a stay of execution, she invites the King and Haman to a banquet. And to prolong things further, she asked for a second banquet the next night before she makes her request.

At this second banquet, she exposes Haman, and the king commands that Haman be impaled on the gallows he built for Mordecai. The lesson here: the gallows prepared for you by others are not for you.

Ahasuerus now goes to Mordecai to see how he should save the Jews. Mordecai was then given the place of Haman as the second in command in the kingdom. God takes care of His people for His people are not excluded from high places.

There are many lessons we should learn from this story of **Queen Esther**:

- First of all, it is not until we believe that one person can make a difference that we will take a risk as Esther did.

- Before she took the risk, she took three days to pray, because prayer works. Prayers give strength, energy, and perspective.

- When we invite others to join us in our battle, they also benefit.

- No king has ever intimidated God. Proverbs 21:1 NASB – *"The king's heart is like channels of water in the hand of the Lord. He turns it wherever he wants."*

- When all seems lost, it is not.

- When no one seems to notice, they do.

- When everything seems great, it may not be.

- When nothing seems just, God is still in control.

- When God seems absent, that is when He is most present.

- God puts us where He wants us to be. You are, right now, exactly where God wants you to be. (1 Thessalonians 5:16-18)

- God will give you the wisdom to know when to speak and when to be silent, just as He did for Esther.

And a few lessons from **Queen Vashti**:

- Looking at a woman with lust is not a compliment. Respect is worth standing up for.

- Beauty is only skin deep. Character is critical.

And a few lessons from **Haman**:

- Revenge does not belong to you. Don't underestimate the power of the pull of revenge.

- Don't overestimate your importance. Don't take your ego to a fight.

- Don't let power go to your head.

God prepares us for the job He wants us to do, and He works on the hearts of others to help us fulfill the jobs He gives us. He will even guide our enemies to cooperate with His plan. His plans are just and fair - even when they don't always seem to be to us; and His plans are not hindered by man. He creates events to give us favor when needed. There will always be someone to resent your worship. The words and His timing will come for us as they did for Esther, if you are paying attention. God's blessings far outweigh anything we can imagine. What man plans for evil, God uses for good. God's purpose is not frustrated by us.

Prayer Works!

John the Apostle

- Father: Zebedee
- Mother: Possibly Salome
- Brother: James
- Partners: James, Peter, Andrew
- Originally a Disciple of John the Baptist
- Born @ 6AD – Died about 100AD – 94 years
- Only disciple to die of old age

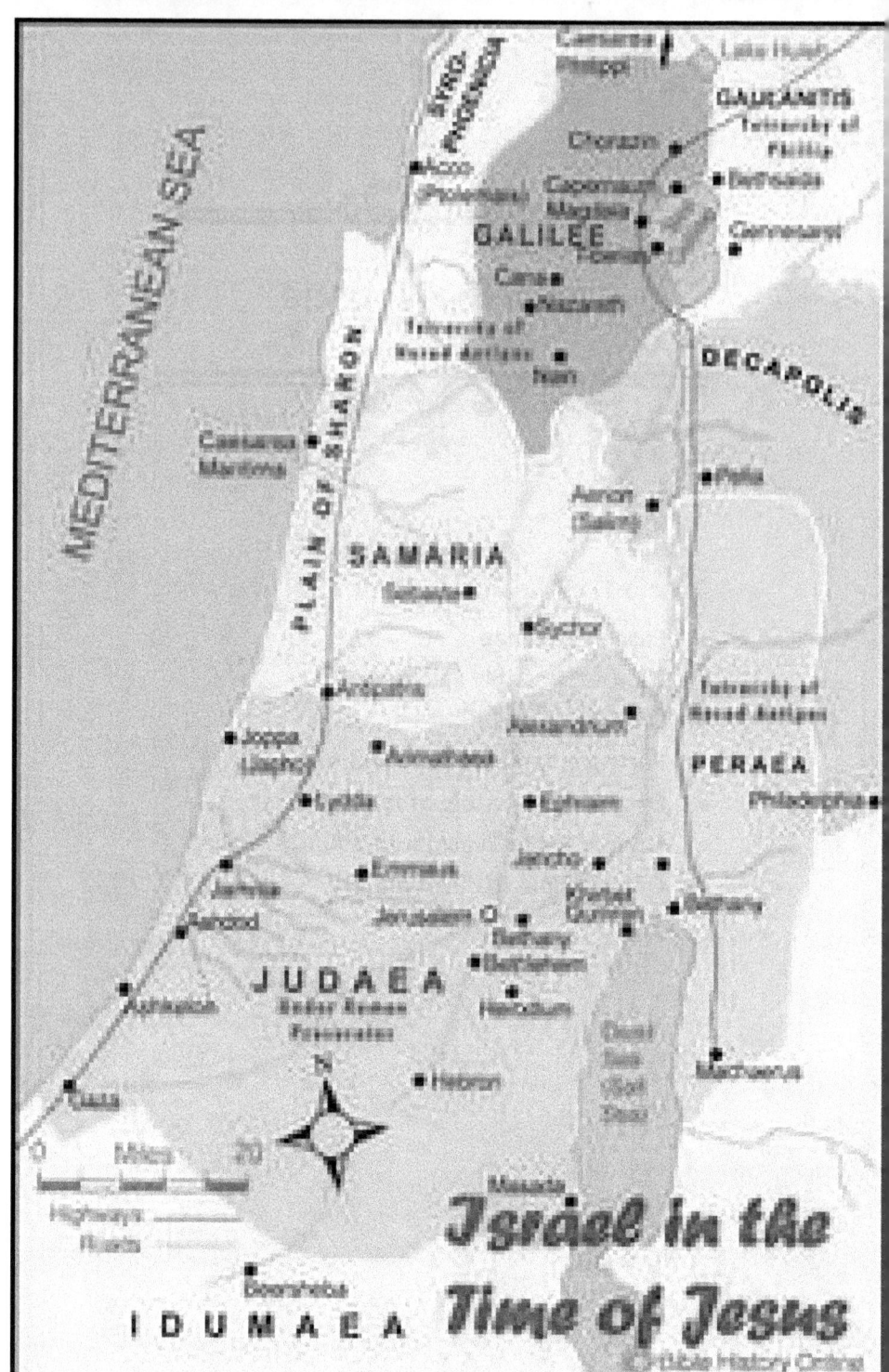

The Book of John is one of the four gospels, probably the last one and written in John's latter years. Had he written it in his younger years, I feel the stories would have been much different. Whereas Matthew, Mark, and Luke focus on Jesus as a man, John focus on Him as God. He was the youngest of all the apostles and, by himself, was considered the favorite of the Lord.

John's father, Zebedee, owned a boat that he and his brother, James, worked on with the servants. This would indicate that John's family was among the wealthier of the people at the time. Peter and Andrew were partners with them, as Peter also owned a boat. And it is recorded that his mother, assumed in history to be Salome, was one of the women who supported Christ financially in His mission.

John traveled with Jesus for 3 ½ years. He was originally a disciple of John the Baptist and apparently met Jesus at the Jordan when Jesus was baptized by John the Baptist. John had Andrew go with him to find out where Jesus lived and was converted to be one of Jesus' disciples. John is the author of the books of John, First John, Second John, Third John, and Revelation and reveals many lessons in the Book of John from the stories he tells of his time with Christ. You will find many miracles in John's first recorded book; six are unique to him only. You will find seven "I AM" statements in John's book. In Jewish writing, the number seven represents complete.

John's book is complete proof of Jesus' divinity.

As a young man, John and his brother James must have had quick tempers as Jesus nicknamed them the "Sons of Thunder." At one point when they are traveling through Samaria the brothers wanted Jesus to rain down thunder and destroy the city for its lack of faith in Him. However, in his later years, John was known as "the elder" and well respected. He went from a son of thunder to a child of God; from praying for destruction to praying for blessings.

You can tell the most about John's character by what he wrote and what he chose to leave out of his writings. In his gospel, he never says a bad word about anyone other than Judas and the devil. (Even when Peter walked on water, John never said that he fell.) As Ellen G. White wrote, *"He yielded his resentful, ambitious temper to the molding power of Christ, and Divine Love wrought in him a transformation of character."* John recognized Christ as the Son of God. He respected Him and loved Him.

When traveling with Jesus, the home base was Capernaum. Later John lived in Ephesus and then was exiled to the island of Patmos for his preachings. It was there that he wrote the book of Revelation; the book that tells us what is to come.

John does not start his writing with the birth of Christ, but with the power of Christ as God. One of his first stories is of the wedding in Cana where Jesus performed His first recorded miracle by turning water into wine – a simple story of Christ's power and compassion on others and His respect for his earthly mother. The lesson we learn from Mary here is to give God the request and leave the solution in His hands. Mary simply said to the servants, "Whatever He says do, do it." She knew He would not let her down.

The Samaritans were a rogue group of Jews that were outcast by the Jews as false worshipers. The Jews had nothing to do with them. Even John and James wanted to destroy the city. But it is when John tells the story of the Samaritan Woman at the well that we start to see a lesson learned by John. First of all, Jesus is speaking to a Samaritan; second of all, Jesus is speaking to a woman. Why? This was unknown to the Jews, so why is Jesus wasting His time here? Apparently, the prejudice of the Jews and His disciples was so great that Jesus had to send the disciples away to buy food so he would have the opportunity to approach the Samaritan woman. There are multiple lessons in this story aside from prejudice. It was here that Jesus had an entire city convert to Him because of the witness of one outcast person.

In his travels with Christ, John comes with Jesus to the pool of Bethesda where he finds a large crowd of people in pain and suffering looking for healing. There they meet a man who had been disabled for 38 years. This time, the man does not ask for help, Jesus just gives it. But He gives it with the instruction to go forward and watch his behavior or what will come will be worse than what he has already suffered. This lesson proved that you cannot out-sin God's forgiveness. Nothing is too hard for God. But He does expect you to do your part.

John goes on to prove his point by telling the story of Jesus feeding 5,000 men plus women and children with two fish and five loaves of bread. Faith in your Higher Power makes a difference and the little one with the lunch, and the disciples, learned sometimes the greatest miracles happen when we give up what we have to help someone else.

When John tells the story of the woman in adultery, he is showing that God gives second chances. That He forgives but expects us to learn from the mistakes. Then, when Jesus heals the man who was born blind, it was to prove the power of God. Nothing like this had ever been done before. Don't give up on God. God uses disabilities to bring people to Him. It may be to bring us, or it may be to bring someone else who is watching us.

Martha and Mary learned to truly trust Jesus when He was "late" getting to their brother, Lazarus. They thought He was late. They were blaming Him for his negligence. Grief often causes us to blame. He knew He was on time. Now the world would have no doubt that He can raise the dead even after four days in the grave. Trust Him in the hard times.

In the final chapters of John, he shows us the Spirit of Christ, the servanthood that He wants us to share. By washing the feet of the disciples, Jesus shows us that even He, being God, would not consider it a burden to wash the feet of those who love Him. We need to actually look for opportunities to serve. Only John recorded the prayer Jesus prayed for his disciples at the last supper. We are loved and we are covered.

As the final hours progress and Peter denies the Lord, it is John that records the time on the beach that Jesus has Peter declare three times that he loves Him. He cleared Peter of his transgression and planted a seed of servanthood in his heart.

It was John at the cross that took Mary, the mother of Jesus, into his home to become her son. Whether Jesus made that request because John was the only one in a position to do so, or whether this was to be another lesson for John, we do not know. But we do know that John lived the rest of his life as the "loved disciple".

Some additional lessons from the Book of John:

- ▶ Help where you can. Even small things make a difference. Water to wine did not save a life, but it certainly made an event.

- ▶ Open your heart to help when you are needed. Providing Christ with water gave the Samaritan woman living water.

- ▶ Sharing brings rewards. The Multitude were fed on a child's lunch.

- ▶ Pay Attention! Your Higher Power shows up when He is needed with lessons you need – often without being asked, as he did in Bethesda!

- ▶ Trust in all circumstances. Nothing is too hard for God. Nothing is impossible for God. Read the story of Lazarus.

- ▶ **ASK GOD.** He loves to give. It proves His power and His love for you.

John goes from story to story and tells us, if all the stories had been told, the world would not have been able to hold them. He wrote three additional personal letters that are recorded and the book of Revelation preparing us for His soon coming. May you enjoy all of them.

Jairus

Matthew 9: 18-26; Mark 5: 21-43: Luke 8: 40-56

- Ruler of the Synagogue: Jairus
- Unknown Woman: Woman with an issue of blood
- Date: 1st Century AD
- Where: Capernaum

In the Jewish society, the Synagogue was the seat of healing, education, and control. If you were put out of the Synagogue, you had a hard time surviving. Jairus was the ruler of the Synagogue. He had the power to put one out of the Synagogue. Therefore, he was one of the most powerful people in Capernaum. He was rich, He was educated, He was in control. People parted ways for him.

But Jairus was blind to the future, just as we are all blind to the future, and he was scared. Jairus was like a blind man begging for a gift. We are all legally blind begging for a gift of mercy from God;

> Rich, Poor,
>> Black, White,
>>> Male, Female,
>>>> Educated, Uneducated
>>>>> Every race, Every Nationality

We do not know what the future brings!

Jairus' 12-year-old daughter was dying, and he had no power to save her. As powerful as he was in the community, he was out of control when it came to saving his child. He was in pain, and his only choice was to humble himself and ask for help from the only One he knew who could give it. He obviously had heard the stories of Jesus ability to heal and, even though the Jews in power were not accepting the fact that Jesus was the Messiah, they could not deny his healing powers.

Jairus would give up all he had just to save his daughter; but all he had would not save her. He had heard about Jesus. He knew He was in town. He believed Jesus could save his daughter; but he is not in a position to barter – he has nothing to barter with. Nothing he had was valuable enough to save his daughter. He was not in a position to negotiate – there was nothing he could offer.

All he could do was plead, not ask, but plead. The only option for this proud man was to beg on bended knees for help from the only one he thought could give it.

There are times when there is nothing we have to offer. No bargain we can make, no negotiation we can commit to get what is important to us, when all we have to offer will not get us what we want. Nothing we have will be enough. All we can do is **Ask God**! All Jairus could do was to ask God for help.

So, Jairus went to Jesus – the one the Synagogue was persecuting. The one the Synagogue was out to kill. But no danger was too great for him to seek the help he knew would work. He went to Jesus and begged Him to come save his child. He knew he did not have a lot of time. Her life was running out. When Jairus finds Christ in a crowd of people, he stops Him, makes his request, and Jesus agrees to follow him.

In that crowd was a woman who had suffered for twelve years with an issue of blood that no doctor could heal. She had spent all she had. She was poor, and because of her issue, she was an outcast from society. But she sincerely believed, if she could just touch the hem of Jesus's robe, she would be healed. So, as Jesus was on the way to Jairus's home, He is interrupted. Someone touched Him and He felt power of healing leave Him; so, He stops. When Jesus stops, Jairus waits. There were many people touching Jesus, but there was one who believed; and because of her belief, she was healed, and Jesus felt it.

As Jesus turns to confront her, He asked her to tell her story publicly; of all the doctors and all the pain and all the embarrassment she has suffered for twelve long years. It is important that those around Jesus know that a miracle has been performed. It is important that they know Jesus can and does heal, and all it takes is belief and asking.

It is bad enough that Jairus' trip is interrupted; but now he has to wait for this woman to tell her whole story. He could not rush Jesus for he was solely dependent upon Jesus for healing. Jairus is in a hurry. Jesus is not. So Jairus waits!

This woman had suffered for twelve years. Jairus' daughter is twelve years old. If Jairus wanted to know how long this woman had suffered, all he had to do was to remember how many years he had with his daughter. But his mind is not on the woman. His mind is on his child. We do the same thing. We have a difficult time thinking of another's problems when ours are so large.

While Christ is talking with the woman, Jairus gets the message from home that it is too late; his daughter has died. God says to us what Christ said to Jairus: "Just Believe and all will be well." These are the times that it is hard to believe. But Jairus had no choice if he wanted his daughter back.

Now Jesus goes from following Jairus to Jairus following Him. Jairus has a choice to make. Does he believe it is too late for Jesus to do anything, or does he believe that Jesus can still heal? As Max Lucado said, *"Faith sometimes begins by stuffing you ears with cotton."* In other words, ignore the rest of the world and just listen to Jesus. Sometimes, when we are at our worst moment, we have to tune out the world and focus only on Jesus. Don't listen to the naysayers who are always spewing negatives. The people said she was dead. Christ ignored them. He knew that was not a problem for Him. He knew what was coming. He knew the future. He knows our future too.

Don't limit your possibilities to the visible.

2 Corinthians 4:18 *"We set our eyes not on what we can see but on what we cannot see. What we see will last only a short time, but what we cannot see will last forever."*

Christ said, *"She is not dead, she is sleeping."* The mourners knew the child had died, and they laughed at Jesus. Obviously, they did not believe that He could raise the dead. Christ went from being worshiped and praised to being ridiculed and laughed at. But Jairus was not laughing. If he was anything like me, he was praying.

So, Jesus cast the mourners out. The Hebrew word used for "to cast out" here is the same word used 38 times in the Bible to cast out Demons. It is the same word used to cast out the moneychangers in the Temple. These were unbelievers. Unbelievers can cast doubt on believers. We have to cast them out in order to protect our faith. Jesus did not ask that they leave. He demanded that they do so.

Where Jairus was afraid of death, Jesus welcomed it. To Jesus this was an opportunity for Him to show what faith could do. This was an opportunity to show the Power of God. It was a chance for Jairus to either live by fact or see by faith.

When Jesus said his daughter was sleeping, He was right. God tells us that death is simply sleep until He returns for His followers. Well over 100 times, the Bible refers to death as sleep (read the story of Lazarus). When we see death, we see disaster. When God sees death, He sees deliverance. Death is supposed to hurt. It is the penalty for sin. But death is a small price to pay to set at His table. From life, to death, to paradise when Christ returns!

In this story, Jesus went from the follower to the guide. As soon as Jairus realized he was no longer in control, he became the follower. To follow Christ paid off for him. He received the precious gift of his child back in his arms just because he believed.

In this story, you will find that Jesus is selective with whom He allows to witness his work. He only allowed the parents and Peter, James, and John to witness the raising of the daughter. It took a while for even his disciples to believe in Him. It may be that these three disciples were the only ones ready to witness this great power.

There are two stories in this story: We have the ruler of the church, Jairus, and the casted-out woman with an issue of blood. Jesus does not play favorites. He treated the rich, educated, powerful man the same way He treated the poor, uneducated, rejected woman. Both were equally important to Him. He accommodated Jairus, and He accommodated her. He served both. God does not play favorites.

Lessons from Jairus:

- Jesus did not rush. His timing was and is always perfect.
- Do not listen to those who do not know the future. Listen to the One who controls it.
- The one who believes in the One who holds the future

does not need to fear it, for the One who controls the future has no fear of it.

- Select your associates carefully. Unbelievers can challenge your faith.
- Be patient. Sometimes we have to have temporary losses to show us the abundance of His blessings.
- Love your neighbor as you love yourself. Be sensitive to the problems of others.
- God has no favorites. He loves each of us equally.
- All we have to do is **ASK**: **A**sk, **S**eek, and **K**nock.

There is a great journal called ***Ask God*** by Deborah Glass. A wonderful tool if you choose to use it. It will allow you to track your prayer requests and record the answers, which gives you a better sense of how God works. Some answers take longer than others, but they all seem to come right on time.

The Apostle Peter

- Father: Jonah
- Brother: Andrew
- Born: 1 AD in Bethesda
- Died: 67 AD in Rome under Nero
- Occupation: Fisherman
- Partners: Zebedee and two sons James and John
- Also known as: Simon (in Hebrew), Cephas (In Aramaic), Petro (or Rock) by Christ

Have you ever been a Peter and done the very thing you said you would not do?

Have you ever gone fishing (or returned to your old life) after a spiritual failure?

Do you question whether you can be forgiven after a betrayal?

If so, you will love the story of Peter!

Peter and his brother, Andrew, were among the first disciples chosen by Jesus. We know that Peter was married and had a son. It is historically assumed that the Book of Mark was written by his son, Mark, as told by Peter. We do not know for sure if Mark was his biological son or spiritual son (as Timothy was to Paul).

As you read the Gospels, you learn that Peter was the outspoken disciple. He was quick to speak, slow to learn, and impulsive. He was not formally educated but was obviously successful for his time. He owned his own boat and was partners with Zebedee and his two sons, James and John, who were also chosen as disciples. And Peter was the first to acknowledge Jesus as the Son of God.

Peter's strength came from his weakness. It was Peter who publicly denied Christ three times when He was being held by the Pharisees, and his shame over that act pushed him to stand up where others did not. When Jesus met Peter on the seashore and Jesus asked him three times if he loved Him - and three times Peter said he did - the transgression was forgiven. There are many different words for Love in the Hebrew language:

- Agape Love = Unconditional Love
- Phileo Love = Brotherly Love

In Christ's first and second question to Peter of "Do you love me", He used the word Agape and Peter responded with Phileo – I love you as a brother. But in his last response,

Peter responded with Agape, "I love you unconditionally". Peter was then instructed to "feed my flock", and he made this his mission for the rest of his life and eventually was martyred for it under the Emperor Nero.

After Christ's resurrection, Peter, Andrew, James, and John, along with the other disciples, became Apostles of the faith and were the leaders that took Christianity to the rest of the world. Peter had the first converts after the Cross when he preached at Pentecost and over 3,000 were converted. He, along with Christ's brother, James, became the leader of the church in the first century, and he never again denied Jesus as the Christ even unto his death.

At the time of Christ crucifixion, Jesus and the disciples were living in the city of Capernaum. After the resurrection, Peter returned to Capernaum and from there traveled throughout the Roman Empire preaching for Christ. He went from Capernaum to Samaria, from Lydda to Joppa, then to Caesarea, Antioch in Syria, to Asia Minor, then to Rome, where, according to the historian Clement, he was crucified upside-down because he said he was not worthy to be crucified as his Lord was.

Map of the Roman Empire 1st Century

Peter was one of only three disciples present with Christ when he raised Jairus' daughter, and he was present at the Transfiguration where he saw Moses and Elijah. He is always the first disciple mentioned when they are listed, which indicates from the traditions of that time that he was the first in importance. After the resurrection, it was Peter who was the first to enter the empty tomb.

Peter is credited as the author of 1 Peter and 2 Peter in the New Testament and is assumed to be the dictator of the book of Mark, which was based on his story. Peter was the preacher to the Jewish people (whereas Paul was assigned the Gentiles). In the Book of 1 Peter, he is writing to forewarn of the persecution that Christians were receiving from the outside, and in 2 Peter, the warning was for the heresy from the inside of the Church. It is assumed Historically that his writings were done to Asia Minor from Rome.

The purpose of all Peter's writing was to show that God calls His people to be holy. This is not our permanent home. We are aliens on this earth, and we will be vindicated in the end. Christ will return so we can be where He is.

Jesus was Peter's mentor. He learned to leave revenge in God's hands. If Jesus, the most powerful of all, could tolerate unmerited abuse, so could he – so can we! Jesus had told him that unlike the Jewish rule of forgive your adversary five times, we should forgive seventy time seven times. In other words, don't keep up with how many, just continue to let go and let God handle the problem.

Peter learned, from Christ washing his feet, that humility is not a feeling. To "feel" humble is not humility. Humility is an action. *"Humility is not thinking less of yourself but thinking of yourself less often."*

Some of the lessons I received from Peter were:

- A promotion is not moving up the ladder, it is moving toward your calling.
- Focus on your own assignment.
- Our best effort at service represents our highest form of gratitude to God. Follow in His footsteps.
- We will have trouble in this world, but we have support.
- Be active, intent, and obedient while you focus on your future in Heaven.
- Distractions take us away from what is important.
- If God said it, it will happen.

Peter went from a foot-in-the-mouth (bold but often wrong) gruff, arrogant, cocky man of impulse to a humble, willing, caring and obedient servant of the Lord – even unto death. He lived for about 65 years and preached for about 33. As he preached, he grew and added the fruits that proved his sincerity: Goodness, Knowledge, Self-control, Perseverance, Affection, and Love.

Peter often had to be corrected, even by Paul, for his prejudice in favor of the Jews. That was his heritage and hard to give up. But he became Christ's cornerstone for the new church because of his deep love for God and His people (all people) by his lessons from Cornelius.

We can be wrong and forgiven. Peter's personality did not change. His control of it did!

Paul
(6AD to 66AD)

- Born: Tarsus, Asia Minor
- Died: Rome, Italy
- Father: Antipater II related to King Herod the Great
- Mother: Cypros
- Nephew: Julius Archelaus (friend of historian Josephus)
- Relatives: Andronicus and Junice (Christians before Paul)
- Teacher: Gamaliel
- Tribe: Benjamin
- Occupation: Tent Maker and leather worker (Romans 16:7)

Saul Paulus was born in about the year 5 or 6AD in the city of Tarsus in Asia Minor, which meant he would have been the same age as the Apostle John. He was surrounded by Gentiles, Romans and Jews and had dual citizenship with the Jews and the Romans. He was awarded Roman citizenship because his family had been among the social elite in the Roman Empire for at least four generations. His father, grandfather, and great-grandfather had been related to the family of Herod the Great.

Tarsus was known as a University City because of the vast library there established in about 300BC by Alexander the Great and because of its dedication to education for its citizens. It was a great city of commerce with a population of about 250,000. Living there, Paul was surrounded by a varied population and blessed with a good education so that he spoke Greek, Roman, and Aramaic languages.

It was common for Jewish children from prominent families to start their education at 5 years old and advance to Jerusalem for further growth at the age of 13. Paul was sent to Jerusalem to live with his sister and nephew at that time (Acts 23:16). It was here that he was introduced to the renowned Rabbi, Gamaliel, and trained at the Hillel Rabbinical School (Acts 22:3).

Most of the details we have on Paul's life come from the Book of Acts in the Bible. We know he was from the tribe of Benjamin, his father and grandfather were Pharisees, and he was being educated, a devout Jew, to be a Pharisee. He was initially called by his Aramaic name of Saul.

His nephew, Julius Archelaus, was a friend of the first century historian, Josephus, and it is assumed this is the source of Josephus historical information on Paul. According to Josephus, Paul's father was Antipater II, a Roman and relative of Herod the Great, and his mother was Cypros, a Jew from Jerusalem. Josephus described Paul as a small man with a prominent head and hooked nose. This description was expanded in the book <u>Acts of Paul and Thecla,</u> written in 150Ad by Thecla who quoted him as: *"A man small of stature with a bold head and crooked legs, well built, with eyebrows meeting and a nose somewhat hooked."* Many of the painters used this description to recreate Paul. Paul was described as smart, determined, and uncompromising in pursuit of his goals.

Additional information on Paul can be found in David Bordon's book (2005) <u>Discover the Power of the Prayers of Paul</u>, where he says that Paul *"teaches us to love a God we cannot see or touch."* Paul never met Jesus in person. He met Him in prayer.

Paul is credited with writing fourteen of the twenty-seven books of the New Testament. Some scholars credit him with writing the Book of Hebrews, but most do not. Paul's books were accepted into the Bible because of his close association with the Apostle Peter and James, the brother of Jesus. For a book to be introduced into the Bible, the author had to be an Apostle or have a link with an Apostle, as Mark did with Peter.

Paul was originally a persecutor of Christians – in essence, a terrorist out to destroy the sect. He pursued the Christians even though his instructor, Gamaliel, said not to engage (Acts 5:35-39). After his conversion on the Road to Damascus (Acts 9:4), Paul became their biggest supporter. About four or five years after his conversion, about 34 AD, Paul traveled back from Damascus to Jerusalem and met with Barnabas who introduced him to the Apostles. Then Barnabas left to go to Antioch to establish a church there.

Paul became a Christian advocate, closely knit with Peter, James, and the other Apostles. He then returned to Tarsus and remained for fourteen years. It is assumed he spent that time studying the Old Testament for signs that Christ fulfilled the Messiah prophecy. At the end of the fourteen years, Barnabas came looking for Paul to get help in Antioch with the new church. It was in Antioch where Jesus' followers were first called Christians, and it was in Antioch that Paul was confirmed that God wanted him to reach out to the Gentiles. He then changed his given Aramaic name of Saul to his Roman name of Paul to fit in well with his calling. It was in Antioch that Paul made the choice to travel all over the known world to teach and preach Christ Jesus as the Messiah.

One of his biggest challenges Paul faced at that time was those of the Jewish faith did not believe a man who died on a cross was worthy of his allegiance. A man who died on a cross was cursed. Therefore, anyone looking at Christ as the long-awaited Messiah was a threat to their belief and Paul was such a man. Therefore, everywhere Paul went, he was attacked and challenged by the Jews in the area who were stuck in their legalism and not wanting a change, and he was accepted by the Gentiles who were so excited that eternity was being opened to them. Paul tells us his philosophy in Romans 13:10, where he states: **"Love does no wrong to a neighbor; therefore, love is the fulfilling of the law."** And God is Love.

It was from Antioch that Paul launched his first of three mission trips. This one is with Barnabas and John Mark (who is recorded in some parts of history as Peter's son and the author of the book of Mark). This trip took them first to Cyprus then to Pamphylia (today in modern Turkey). It is here we see Paul's first miracles (exercising the evil spirit from the sorcerer, Elymas) and many signs and wonders. And it is here we see Paul's position change from following Barnabas to leading the mission. John Mark chose here to return to Jerusalem and Paul took this as an insult and failure on John Mark's part, causing a drift in his relationship with Barnabas.

On Paul's second mission trip, Barnabas wanted John Mark to join them, but Paul refused to allow him to go. So, Barnabas left with John, Mark, and Paul, chose Silas as his traveling companion. (We do see Paul and John Mark reconcile later, and we see Timothy enter the picture on the second mission.)

Paul's third mission trip went from Galatia, Phrygia, and Ephesus to Corinth. At a stopping point in Toras, one of his young followers fell from a three-story window and died, and, petitioning God for help, Paul raised him back to life. Paul continued on and then, in about 60AD, he headed back to Jerusalem.

The more attention Paul received, the more upset the Jews

became. They hated that he served the Gentiles, and they harassed him everywhere he went. When he finally returned to Jerusalem, they attacked him for the final time, and he ended up in prison and sent to Caesarea for his protection. There he witnessed before Felix and Festus, and King Agrippa before petitioning to go to Rome as a Roman Citizen rather than return to Jerusalem for the Jews to try him.

God had told Paul that he would testify in Rome. He did not have any idea that it would be from a prison cell. When Paul was sent to Rome, he was assigned to the Centurian Julius, and Luke the Physician was allowed to travel with him. On the way, the ship they were sailing in weathered a storm and was beached and broken apart. Because Julius refused to kill the prisoners, Paul's life was saved and when the storm season ended, he was sent on to Rome under in-house arrest. He was under arrest for about two years with a little freedom and then transferred to the dungeon for three years before his death.

It is recorded in history that Paul wrote the Books of Ephesians, Philippians, Colossians, and Philemon under house arrest, as well as Timothy 1 and 2, and Titus from the prison cell.

Three historians (Josephus 37AD to 100AD; Philo of Alexandria 50AD; and Nicephorus 1256-1335AD) reported that Paul was beheaded in Rome in about 66AD.

This is a very short synopsis of fourteen Books of the Bible. There is no possibility that I covered it all. You will have to read for yourself to get all the messages, and all the lessons Paul has to offer. I would suggest you start with the book of Acts.

"God in His divine wisdom and grace exposed Paul to a wide spectrum of experiences and education giving the Apostle to the Gentiles the tools he needed to effectively spread the Gospel and establish the church solidly in all parts of the Roman Empire." From <u>The Early Life and Background of Paul the Apostle</u> by Rev. Quency E. Wallace (2002) <u>www.biblicaltheology.com</u>

If we take the time to look back in our own lives, we will find that God has done the same for us. He has placed us where He wants us to be and given us the tools we need to accomplish the plan He has for our lives. It is up to us to work with Him to achieve His goal.

Paul's story teaches us we cannot be too bad for God to forgive us. He can use us no matter what is in our background. He can take us from our wrong decisions and make us right with Him. Remember, God has a plan for every life He creates, but He gives us the choice of whether to follow His lead or not. I pray that these studies will encourage you to dig in and discover the golden nuggets God has specifically for your life.

After Thoughts

This book was written to entice you to get excited about the Bible and all God has to offer us in it. Some parts of the Bible are difficult to understand and some of the war stories are hard to read; but, **with prayer**, your persistence, tenacity, self-discipline and determination will reap many rewards. Prayer will be the ultimate answer to all your problems, for God does answer prayer. But praying is a challenge on several levels. First, we don't always get the answer we want to get, or we don't get it as fast as we think we should, and we think God is not listening. And, often, we blame God for the challenges in our life that do not come from him; then we think he is unjust or unkind; and, therefore, we don't pray!

We ask God for what He cannot give without violating

another's rights. We each have the right to choose, and God will not take choice away from us or another. Therefore, if we ask Him to change someone else's mind, He will not do that; but He will do for us exactly what He said He would do. He will honor Romans 8:28 *"All things work for good for those who love the Lord and are called according to His purpose."* The answer you receive will be better than the request you made.

For those of you who don't pray because you don't think you know how to pray, I love this quote from Max Lucado:

"Just as a happy child cannot mis-hug, the sincere heart cannot mis-pray. Heaven knows, life has enough burdens without the burden of praying correctly. If prayer depends on how I pray, I'm sunk. But if the power of prayer depends on the One who hears the prayer, and if the One who hears the prayer is my Daddy, then I have hope. Prayer really is that simple. Resist the urge to complicate it."

As you read and study your Bible, you will receive instruction on how to pray, what to pray for, and what your responsibility is in getting your prayers answered. Prayers do not need to be spoken out loud or shared with anyone. Oswald Chambers, in his book **Run Today's**

Race, states: *"Jesus did not say 'dream about your Father in secret,' but **'pray** to thy Father in secret.' Prayer is an effort of will. After we have entered our secret place and have shut the door, the most difficult thing to do is to pray. The great battle in private prayer is the overcoming of mental wool-gathering."*

Pick a special time and place where you will not be distracted or interrupted and pour your heart out to your God. Then wait and be receptive to the answer He will give. It may take a while to understand the answer; but it will always be better than anything you could ask for.

www.ingramcontent.com/pod-product-compliance
Lightning Source LLC
Chambersburg PA
CBHW071726090426
42738CB00009B/1896